Minnesota Memories 7

Joan Claire Graham & 44 Friends

Before movies, radio, television and the Internet, people spent millenniums perfecting the art of storytelling. The world's oldest form of entertainment owes its longevity to its simplicity and to the timeless appeal of a well-told story. Unlike news reporters who hit readers in the first paragraph with all they really need to know, a storyteller unfolds events like a screenplay with an establishing shot, story exposition, ascending action, conflict, climax and resolution.

As I travel around Minnesota, talking to people and inviting them to send me their best true stories to share with the world in the *Minnesota Memories* book series, I am always impressed by their knowledge, their instinctive need to share what they know, and their innate ability to choose a storytelling style that will evoke a response from their intended audience, whether that response is laughter, understanding, sympathy, empathy, nostalgia, or amazement at unusual things that really happen.

Hollywood screenwriters have spent thousands of highly-paid hours inventing some crazy Minnesota stories and characters. Rose of *The Golden Girls* was the stupid one, Jerry Lundegaard in *Fargo* was a bungling crook, and Ted Baxter on *The Mary Tyler Moore Show* demonstrated how inept a newsman could be—if he was broadcasting from Minneapolis. When I moved away to other states and told people I was from Minnesota, they looked sympathetic and started talking slower. Convincing them to ignore those media-made stereotypes and believe that Minnesota people are actually intelligent, hard-working, good-humored, highly educated, creative and resourceful people was difficult.

So I decided to give genuine Minnesota people, who do such a good job of storytelling, a chance to show the world what we're *really* like by writing and publishing their own true stories. These are not Ole and Lena jokes, nor do they contain hot dish lore or the phrase "you betcha." *Minnesota Memories* are real stories by real Minnesota people, and reading them is just a lot more fun than a person ought to be able to have. If this is your first *Minnesota Memories* volume, welcome aboard, and if you like this book, check out the six that preceded it.

Joan Claire Graham, Purveyor of Memories

Do you have a true story to submit for *Minnesota Memories 8?*

Send your true stories for the next volume.

**Minnesota Memories
439 Lakeview Boulevard
Albert Lea, Minnesota 56007
or email them to MinnMemory@aol.com.**

To book a program for your organization, library, store, church, historical society, class reunion, writers' group, or school call 507-377-1255.

To learn more about *Minnesota Memories* or to order additional copies or previous volumes, call, write or visit our website,
www.MinnesotaMemories.com

Minnesota Memories 7
Copyright 2007, Graham Megyeri Books
All Rights Reserved.
No portion may be reprinted or copied without publisher's permission.

Most photographs were taken and provided by contributors.

Cover photo by Aquinata "Cookie" Graham. Thanks, Mom!
Back cover photo by Leah Nell Peterson, Cannon Falls Beacon

ISBN: 978-0-9791994-1-7

Minnesota Memories 7

Contributors	Page	Hometowns & Story Settings
Louise M. Aamodt	158	Lakeville
Elizabeth Becker	54	Victoria, Minneapolis
Carolyn Light Bell	112	Minneapolis
Tom Butsch	27	Minneapolis, Shakopee
Lin Calof	67	Minneapolis, Grand Marais
Pauline Danforth	56	White Earth Reservation, Minneapolis
Lloyd Deuel	70	Foreston
Janet Anhorn Gaughran	99	Austin, Jordan
Joan Claire Graham	7	Albert Lea, Hayward, Other Places
Amanda Elizabeth Haldy	174	Becker
Richard Hall	50	Austin
Esther Haraldson	89	Brook Park, Shoreview
Mike Harvey	96	Pelican Rapids, Grand Forks
Dave Healy	103	St. Paul
Alyce Jacobsen	75	Spring Valley, Albert Lea
Mary Kalkes James	101	Northfield
Ken Jenkins	155	Itasca, Manchester, Kiester, Albert Lea
Muriel Johnson	46	Lake Bronson
Patricia Kniefel	189	Sherburn
Robert D. "Cobb" Knutson	205	Albert Lea
Betsy Leach	164	Scandia, St. Paul
Carol Keech Malzahn	109	Sveadahl, Minnesota Lake
Kimberly Mark	160	Forest Lake, Grand Rapids
Don Matejcek	203	Owatonna
Kathy Megyeri	37	Owatonna
Kathy Moe	146	Springfield, Clements
Kathryn L. Nelson	35	Minneapolis, Osseo
Ken Nelson	78	Gunflint Trail, Albert Lea
Mary Murphy Ottum	196	Esquagamah, Aitkin
Lorna Rafness	124	Minneota, Mankato
Harvey Ronglien	65	Owatonna
Wendy Skinner	61	St. Louis Park
Stella Sorbo	118	Two Harbors, Freeborn
Ted Springer	130	Minneapolis
Dennis Stern	182	Minneapolis, Ivanhoe
Alice Stielow	85	Clinton
Mary Stoesz	44	Elko
Steve Swanson	42	Northfield, Minnetonka Mills
John Tripp	142	Austin, Duluth, Minneapolis
Anastasia Vellas	136	Swatara
Robert Walsh	94	Belle Plaine, Cannon Falls
Dex Westrum	169	Albert Lea, Faribault
Marian Westrum	134	Albert Lea
Gloria Wilkinson	92	Oklee, Parkers Prairie, Fergus Falls
Julie Zappa	139	East St. Paul

Minnesota Memories 7

Table of Contents

The Stories That Never Got Written…7
All I Want for Christmas is My Two Front Teeth…11
The Lady in the Window…15
Goodbye to a Small Town Hardware Store…18
July 18, 1995: Sisyphus and the Hide-a-Bed…22

The Stagecoach Opera House in Shakopee…27
Mabel for Strongest Woman…35
Daniel Gainey, a Minnesotan Who Affected My Life…37
How I Became a Recycler…42
Taking Care of Shetland Ponies…44

The Big Storm of April 1997…46
Transportation and Commerce…50
Twenty Years Later, Return to the U of M…54
Fry Bread Love…56
Marsh Secret…61
I Hope She's Not Still Waiting…65

Snowshoeing the Kadunce…67
Wintertime During the Depression…70
Crossing Deer Creek…75
Ice Golfing…78
There Must Be a Better Way to Shot a Deer…80
A Short Tie Affair…83
The Nettle Patch…85
Fighting Fire…89
The Sting of Honey…91

It All Started in My Bedroom…92
Serving Mass on Christmas Eve 1943…94
Unplanned Family Reunion at the Lake…96
Tunney…99
The Klan…101

Minnesota Memories 7
Table of Contents Continued...

The Green Parking Lot...103
Newcomer to a Small Town...109
Paperboy...112
Joys of Jule-bokking...118
Important Lessons My Parents Taught Me...121

Memories of My Country School–District #27...124
Lunch With Grandma...128
Sundays With My Folks...130
World War II Jobs for Women...134
My First Pair of Skis...136

The Alleys Were Magical...139
When Bigfoot Lurked in Austin...142
Farm Chores...146
Mother's Legacy...150
Growing up in the Depression and War Years...155

The Frosty Trap...158
Hooked...160
Poop and Coop, Inc....164
Albert Lea Country Club: Goodbye to All That...169
Snow Angels...174
Travels With My South Minneapolis Softball Gang...182

Bean Walking in Southern Minnesota...189
The Life of a Newspaper Carrier...193
The Fire in Esquagamah...196
Esquagamah Country Teachers...200
Gear Head...203
Victory Can Be Painful...205

How to Submit a Story for *Minnesota Memories 8*...207
Minnesota Memories 7 Contributors' Map...208

The Stories That Never Got Written
By Joan Claire Graham

As I travel around the great state of Minnesota telling folks about the importance of writing their stories and gathering true stories for my *Minnesota Memories* book series, people often come up to me after my talk or phone me after a radio interview and tell me a story of their own. My reply is usually, "That really *is* a good story. You should write it and send it to me for the next book."

Usually the person who has approached me announces an intention to do just that, but often this intention gets put on the back burner until it boils dry. When in the process of pulling together material for the next book, I often wish I had some of those stories because I would publish them, thereby giving the world some entertainment or education and the storytellers a chance to become part of recorded Minnesota history.

After I spoke on WCCO radio one night with Al Malmberg, three or four listeners contacted me with stories. One was a farmer from the southwestern part of the state, but I don't remember the town. He told me about one of those early snowstorms that blew in and surprised people who just the day before had been raking leaves and picking pumpkins. This was a fast-moving weather front that started with rain, and before you knew it, turned to sleet and ice.

A farmer's main concern at a time like that is the safety of his livestock, so this guy went out to bring in the cows and calves before they froze to death. As he was thus engaged in his pasture, fighting to stay on his feet because of the virulent wind, his eyes nearly frozen shut from driving sleet, he noticed a couple of pheasants that had been caught off guard by Mother Nature's unseasonable surprise. The birds were frozen stiff, their feathers splayed out where they lay on the ground, encrusted with ice.

"Hmmm," he thought. "This looks like supper, and they have nice, clean carcasses because I didn't even have to fire a shot." He picked up the birds and put them into a gunnysack he had been using to wipe down the calves. On his next trip into the barn, he dropped the sack, intending to come back when his work was done to clean the pheasants.

The thought of pheasant for supper sustained him as he did what he needed to do, and when all his livestock was secure and he was fatigued and frozen from the effort it took, he returned to the spot where he had dropped the sack. Much to his surprise, the sack was empty. As he scratched his head trying to figure out if he was looking at the right gunnysack, his gaze drifted over to another part of the barn. There, pecking away at whatever they could find to peck away at, were the pheasants. "I didn't have the heart to kill them," he told me, "not after what they'd been through." He went inside and ate something else for supper, and when the storm abated, he set them free.

A woman had called in to the radio show that same night and told the story about how she and her sister devised what they thought was an innovative way to go fishing. Across their river was a little footbridge with wooden rails for safety. On one of the rails was a knothole so she and her sister thought it would be nifty to stick the baited hook and line through the hole and drop the line into the river. Nothing happened for quite a while, but finally the kids felt a strong pull on the line. It was such a big fish for little girls to handle that they had to work quite hard to reel it in, and they thought they were doing well, but when they had reeled the fish within reach, they faced a problem they hadn't anticipated. The fish was on the outside of the knothole, and the kids were on the other. They couldn't reach over the top because they were too little, and they couldn't reach between the rails because–well, they just couldn't manage.

As the fish struggled, one girl held the line while the other went to find an adult to give them a hand. Help arrived, but they never heard the end of it. "What were you girls thinking? A fish couldn't fit through that tiny hole! Don't you have the brains you were born with?" In the old days, that was a question some adults felt entitled to ask little kids when they did things that weren't all that smart.

From the sound of her voice, I would guess that the woman had been telling this story for a few decades, but she never wrote it down and sent it to me. WCCO listeners heard it that night, and we had a good laugh in the studio. I wish I could write her name here and give her credit, because she and everybody else can see that it's a pretty good story. It probably reminds us all of something similarly silly we did as kids.

I've been on his show a few times, and Al Malmberg always says, "I'll have to write the story about our senior prank at Richfield High School." Some tires or wheels ended up at the base of the flagpole, looped over the top, but he never wrote and divulged the secret about how he and his fellow seniors executed that prank. Perhaps he will some day.

A friend of mine in St. Louis Park used to start all conversations with, "I'll have to send you my stories about the caves around Winona." His Christmas card notes used to contain written verification of his intention to send me those stories, but he seems to have gotten over that notion because after five years he's stopped bringing up the topic, and I've given up hope. Maybe he's saving those cave stories for a bestseller he intends to write someday.

Contributor Stacy Vellas recently wrote from California and said, "People just won't write their stories. You have to do it for them." I disagree. Maybe some won't, but many will–if they have the motivation. In seven *Minnesota Memories* books, I have published hundreds of stories written by hundreds of contributors. Offshoots from this project, *Albert Lea Remembers* and *Austin Remembers*, have yielded an additional 250 stories. The Friends of the Library in Lake City put together their own book of community stories and so did the people of Springfield.

Writing your story is the only way to ensure that it will be saved correctly. Do you remember that old party game where one person whispers a message to next person and the whispered story goes around the table? By the time it gets back to where it started, the story is barely recognizable. Once you write it down, the story is set in stone.

People sometimes raise eyebrows when I say that contributing their stories provides a chance to be a part of recorded history. How could a story about your teacher, your childhood treasures, or one about a funny predicament be considered history? Descriptions of bygone times, anecdotes of daily life and emotional tributes are not found in history books that mainly deal with wars, economic trends, territorial expansion and disasters. *Minnesota Memories* are stories of ordinary things that helped build the foundation of our lives, and these stories provide testimony of our experience and proof of our cultural values.

My daughters attended a California school that used an assimilation called "Dig" to teach kids about history and anthropology. Two upper grade classrooms formed two teams, and each team cooperatively created a make-believe society. They invented an alphabet, a religion, a government system, a set of social mores, clothing styles, cooking methods and other practical and philosophical elements. Then they made artifacts to reflect their society's systems and values—a rune stone, religious statues, dolls, awards, and other items, and buried their artifacts in the schoolyard.

Each team dug up the other team's artifacts, took them back to their own classrooms, and tried to figure out the other society, based on the clues provided. After a week, both teams presented their findings at a big meeting in the auditorium, where spokespeople presented their interpretations. In some matters, such as the alphabet, both teams were right on the mark. But in other cases, such as social and religious practices, there were some wild misinterpretations. The lesson the kids learned was that whenever people need to decode information based on mere clues, there's a chance they might get it wrong. To ensure that others will understand, you have to spell it out clearly.

I wish I could remember all the stories people told me but forgot to write down, but unfortunately only a few remain clear enough to repeat. I hope I have done justice to these stories that were never written, and I hope Minnesota people continue sending me stories for this book series.

If you want to make a contribution to recorded Minnesota history, here's your chance, and you may not get another one. Because of the capability of computer search engines, future genealogists will find something about each storyteller that goes beyond what they will be able to find by looking at an obituary or courthouse and cemetery records. This is the perfect place to preserve your best true stories.

But my desire to publish your story is not entirely for your benefit, or for the entertainment of readers or for the sake of Minnesota history or to help future genealogists. Not entirely. I must be honest. I enjoy what I do, and I'd like to continue publishing *Minnesota Memories* books until all the great Minnesota stories have been written or until I conk out— whichever happens first.

All I Want for Christmas is My Two Front Teeth
By Joan Claire Graham

It makes sense that in my dotage I have become the self-appointed "purveyor of memories" because I have been blessed with an excellent memory of people, circumstances and incidents of bygone times. I can't remember where I put my keys fifteen minutes ago, but I can remember things that happened when I was a baby. When I look at my First Communion picture, I can recall all the kids' names, even though it's been more than a half-century since I've seen most of them. I remember the names of all my teachers, the answers to the questions in Father McGuire's *New Baltimore Catechism*, the words to all those Ricky Nelson songs, and even the four-digit phone numbers of my childhood friends.

I recall chewing paint off my crib rails with my bottom two teeth. Mother was concerned about the unsightliness of the crib, but she should have been concerned about a baby eating paint. The lead in that paint probably cost me a few IQ points.

Perhaps my earliest memory that makes a good story is of a time before I could talk very much. I remember waking up from an afternoon nap, getting bored with stripping paint, and climbing out of my crib. With my curls stuck to my hot little head, and wearing a pair of red overalls handed down from my brother, I toddled across the room and started down the first of ten steps to our stairway landing. I made more headway than I'd planned with that first step because I fell head over heels, hit the landing, and let out a wail that brought Mother running. She scooped me up and held me close as she rocked and shushed me.

More surprised than hurt, I howled as I snuggled against Mother's ample bosom, her heart beating against my ear. She cooed and patted my back, the way any mother would, and I loved the warmth, affection and attention that this little mishap had earned me. As my comfort and security level returned, I stopped crying and she loosened her grip and became relieved and distracted. Hating to relinquish the hold I had on her attention, with all its attendant details, I revved up my noise machine again. She responded as I hoped she would, but when I cranked up my siren a third time, she held me at arm's length, laughed and said, "You're fine, you little stinker."

My parents always said I was not an easy child, and since I never got in trouble at school or with the law, I think they meant that I did things that made great stories to tell afterwards. Without conflict there is no story so I guess my curiosity and childish ways created conflict. I climbed, I got into things, I spilled paint, broke dishes, tore my clothes, said words that embarrassed my parents and, as if that wasn't bad enough, I had spunk.

Another vivid early childhood memory is of a series of events that occurred on a sunny day in Albert Lea in 1948, when I was 2 years old. Mother was scrubbing the kitchen floor, and to keep me high and dry gave me a piece of pie and put me in my highchair–an old white wooden one with a tray that swung up and over the back to form what they used to call a "youth chair." I wasn't yet a youth, so the tray stayed in front of me as Mother scrubbed and I ate pie. When I finished the pie, I hollered to get down, but the floor was still wet and Mother wanted to keep me contained. She took the plate and fork away but left me where I was.

Then the mail came sailing through the slot on the door so she put down her mop and walked out to the porch to pick it up. Bored and restless as most toddlers would be at that point, with nothing to eat and nowhere to go, I turned around in my seat and checked out the calendar hanging on the wall. It had a little paper pocket beneath the calendar sheets, and Mother had put a clothespin in that pocket. I grabbed the clothespin and started hollering and banging on the high chair tray, protesting my predicament, and Mother said, "In a minute! Hold your horses!"

But my horses were not to be held. If she was going to read mail and scrub floors, I was just going to have to take the bull by the horns and liberate myself. Putting the clothespin in my mouth, I squirmed my hips free of the highchair, stood up on the seat, and then stepped up to the tray. The highchair toppled over forward, I flew through the air, and my clothespin-filled mouth struck the floor, gouging out my two bottom teeth. Blood was everywhere.

Mother scooped me up, cried and screamed, and tried to put my teeth back in. She called Dr. Barr, and he told her to bring me right in. She wrapped the teeth in a handkerchief, popped me into my Taylor Tot stroller, and charged up Water Street, across the tracks, up the high school hill, through Central Park, across three flat blocks on Clark Street and around the corner at Newton to sprint the last block to the doctor's office in the Hyde Building. She wasn't a lightning bolt by nature, so I know she set a personal record for running the 8-block dash. Dr. Barr sat me up on a big table and tested my reflexes, took my temperature and generally checked me out. He was concerned about head trauma because I had fallen from a height of more than three feet and knocked out two teeth.

He looked at those little teeth with their surprisingly big roots wrapped in a bloody handkerchief and told Mother to go across the street to see Dr. Gandrud, the dentist. Dr. Barr had probably called and warned him that we were coming. Mother's anxiety level increased as this odyssey unfolded, and at this point she was far more upset than I was.

Dr. Gandrud checked to see if there were any roots broken, and when he determined that there were not, told my mother the blunt truth. There was nothing for him to do, and I would have to spend the next three or four years without my two front teeth.

In a rare, impractical show of public emotion, Mother rejected this verdict. Couldn't they make a little plate for me? Little false teeth? Wasn't there someone in town who could do that? Without front teeth, I'd develop a lisp and not be able to whistle. Worse yet, I'd never be able to eat an apple! I don't know why she assigned such importance to eating apples because we didn't have an apple tree, and most apples I ate were mushy ones that had been preserved in jars, but in her darkest moments of recalling this experience, she repeatedly expressed sympathy that I would miss out on the childhood experience of eating apples. She was too upset to realize that knocking out those teeth had actually *solved* one of her problems. I could no longer chew paint off my crib rails.

That weekend we drove to Mankato to visit Grandma Sal because two weeks earlier I had posed for some pictures at Mankato's Penny Pictures photo studio. Mother's consolation was that she would at least have those pictures, taken just a few days before my disfiguring accident. But do you know what? Although I smiled in a big way for all five shots on the strip, you could not even see my bottom front teeth. They were as good as gone before I knocked them out!

I wish I could say that I learned my lesson and never climbed again, but such was not the case. My early years continued with the usual number of bumps and bangs, and Mother's histrionic prediction that I would miss out because of no front teeth turned out to be folly. With 18 baby teeth instead of 20, I ate apples, talked without a lisp and learned to whistle.

Later that year, when the song "All I Want for Christmas is my Two Front Teeth" by Spike Jones and His City Slickers became a big hit, my grandmother bought me the record, and I learned all the words, hammed it up, and sang it for the amusement of visitors and family members. Talk about capitalizing on misfortune!

When I was in kindergarten I noticed one day that some little jaggedy teeth were poking through. By that time my two top teeth were gone so the new ones came in handy. Everyone had calmed down long before that time and agreed that as childhood calamities go, mine was hardly worth mentioning. Years later when my mom talked about the day I knocked my teeth out, she was amazed that I remembered so many details and had such a clear chronology of what happened when. I was barely 2 years old, but I guess some experiences just stick with me. Now if I could just remember where I put my keys......

Although I smiled on all five shots, my bottom teeth could not be seen. They were as good as gone!

The Lady in the Window
By Joan Claire Graham

My friend Carol Bergen and I walked home from St. Theodore's school in Albert Lea every day, west four blocks on Clark Street, past the Ford dealership, the VFW, Interstate Power, Ray's Barbershop, Unique Cleaners, Coast to Coast and Gamble's hardware, Russell's Toyland, Thompson Dairy, Shea's Ice Cream, Busy Bee Shoe Repair, the Tot Shop, Morris Furniture, the Avalon Cafe and Christianson's Photography. One might think that a four-block walk through the northern edge of downtown would become old hat for two schoolgirls after seven or eight years, but we always managed to find fascinating and enjoyable distractions.

Sometimes we'd cross the street to Gretchen's Sweets, where Mrs. Emstad hand-dipped caramel corn and caramel apples in a vat located in a recessed window where kids could stand to get a good look. What a sensory smorgasbord! First we'd see molten caramel in the window, then we'd open the door and simultaneously hear the little bell tinkle and smell popcorn and candy, and finally, if I had managed to find five cents under the chair cushion where Dad always reclined and fell asleep after supper as change slid from his pockets, I would taste fresh, warm caramel.

Mother always wondered why it took so long for me to walk home, and it was hard to explain. The time we spent looking at toys in Russell's or admiring clothes on the mannequins in the Tot Shop window or the pictures the photographer displayed went by so fast we lost track of it. I would not dream of telling her that we sometimes ducked through the line of high school guys standing on the little step in front of Shea's and went inside for ice cream. Restaurant workers went on strike once, and people carrying signs picketed the Avalon. That was too interesting to ignore so instead of walking around them, we stood for several minutes and watched pickets walk back and forth.

But there was one impediment to the quick walk home that made the others pale by comparison. In 1953, before everyone had television, Morris Furniture Store staged a live commercial in their window display, and this proved to be so interesting that we not only watched it, time after time, but we told our friends who walked home on other streets to come over to Clark Street to see this incredible show.

A loudspeaker enabled sidewalk spectators to hear, and Carol and I wormed our way up to the front so we could see through the big window. The set consisted of a bed, equipped with a Sealy Posturepedic mattress. I had never heard those words before, but to this day it's the only mattress brand or model I can name off the top of my head. Wearing pajamas, a beautiful young actress stretched, yawned, and got into bed and enacted a peaceful night's sleep as spectators heard a voice explain the benefits of the revolutionary Sealy Posturepedic. The actress woke up well rested, took the microphone, showed us a cross-section model of the mattress, and explained why the Sealy Posturepedic was so comfortable and good for your back. She talked about the price and invited everyone to come inside the store to check out a Sealy for themselves.

It was beyond fascinating. It was unprecedented good fortune to find professionally-produced free entertainment on Clark Street or anywhere else in town, and we were mesmerized. Carol and I were in second grade, and we stood enraptured in front of this live infomercial day after day, and I arrived home extra-late whenever I had a chance to watch and admire the beautiful lady in the window. If there was a crowd, the actress would repeat the show after a few spectators moved away and some new ones arrived. There was always a crowd at school dismissal time so we sometimes stood through two or three enactments of the Sealy Posturepedic mattress demonstration.

The script was always the same, and I was a quick study, so after a couple of days I was able to recite and re-enact the entire thing for my mother. I don't know if she ever saw the real demonstration, but she did buy a Sealy mattress when the time came to replace her old one.

For over a half century I thought I might be the only person in Albert Lea who remembered this story. Two years ago, however, I ran into Mick Kenis at the new Morris Furniture Store, and I asked him about it. His family has owned the business for several decades, and he is nearly my age. Yes indeed, he assured me, a Minneapolis actress had been hired, and she stayed with his family during her Albert Lea engagement. They sold a lot of mattresses because of her, but never replicated the Sealy live-action commercial. Most people were buying television sets by then, and a TV ad could be seen by thousands of people instead of dozens who gathered outside a store window.

Whenever I think about that lady in the window, I remember the television series *That Girl*, in which an aspiring New York actress played by Marlo Thomas accepted outrageous gigs on the periphery of show business that included dressing up like a mop and standing outside a restaurant wearing a chicken suit. I wonder if the Sealy gig launched or squelched the show business career of Albert Lea's storefront actress. I wonder if she went to other towns demonstrating Sealy mattresses in other windows throughout Minnesota while staying in the homes of those other store owners. I wonder if she enjoyed doing it as much as I enjoyed watching her. It ranks as one my most unusual childhood memories, and it certainly must have been one of her most unusual jobs.

Goodbye to a Small Town Hardware Store
By Joan Claire Graham

The village of Hayward, six miles east of Albert Lea, would have probably died in infancy had it not been for someone—whoever it was—who saw an opportunity and a need to build the hardware store that has stood on the corner of Main and Second since 1900.

In the early days, farmers, housewives, handymen, trandesmen, merchants and kids who needed screen doors, oil cans, wagon wheels, cup hooks, frying pans, bicycle tires, claw tooth hammers, barbed wire, carving knives, kite string, barn paint, nuts and bolts, saw blades, cookie jars, drill bits, plungers and hundreds of other practical supplies would have had to have taken a 12-mile round trip to Albert Lea with their horse and wagon. That would have eaten up a good share of the day, so the hardware store became an important community asset.

Before modern forms of transportation, school consolidations, the proliferation of big box stores, and long before the Internet, every little town had a hardware store, a school, a grain elevator, a café, a saloon, and a place to buy groceries. Hayward had all these things too, but they are slipping away as the third millennium charges ahead. The school closed in 1982, and then the grocery store downsized to sell only meat. The most recent casualty of the modern age was the hardware store that closed at the end of March, 2007.

The Hayward Hardware Store

Leo Aeikens became the store's fourth owner in 1983, when the name of the store became Leo's Hardware Hank. Leo grew up on a farm near Maynard and later taught high school German so his problem solving and communication skills, along with his traditional German work ethic, served Hayward well during the quarter century he ran the store.

A step into the store provided a history lesson because Leo ran it much the same way it had been run for more than a century. Six days a week he sat under a pressed tin ceiling at the original stainless steel counter in the back, listening to music or politics on the radio, working the occasional crossword puzzle and reading the daily newspaper, flanked by an old cash register, a roll-top desk, an antique safe, and a display case that once held ammunition and knives.

Wooden and metal shelves, organizer bins and pegs for fasteners, pipes, fittings, hinges, knobs and other stuff held modest amounts of just about everything a person would ever need. There were no fancy display units, scanners or surveillance cameras. Leo didn't take Mastercard or Visa, but the he kept ledger books, and Hardware Hank customers could still buy on credit and settle up at the end of the month.

When a customer entered, Leo greeted him or her by name and gave old-fashioned service and helpful advice. If he or she was trying to figure something out, Leo would draw upon his experience to help solve the problem. He would customize paint colors, help calculate areas and amounts, and search for the right sized piece. If he did not have what was needed, he would offer to order it or even suggest where else the customer might look.

While all this was happening, Leo's Hardware Hank served as an information hub for the town of Hayward. If a baby was born or a wedding was to take place, Leo heard about it and told others. If someone was planning to retire, take a vacation, build an addition or get a hip replaced, Leo and his customers took an interest and updated one another on the progress.

Leo's Hardware Hank continued to serve a necessary purpose for many years, and Leo earned a decent living and sent his son to college. But the demise of the family farm and the evolution of modern retail practice took its toll on small town businesses in recent years.

In the mid 1980s, farmers around Hayward still raised dairy cattle and other livestock, but since that time the number of dairy farms in Freeborn County has dropped from 200 to 19. Family farmers who worked 365 days a year to sustain their immediate families and make a contribution to the nation's breadbasket once provided the mainstay of Leo's sales. But they grew old, died or retired, and those who bought their land had a new outlook. Factory farmers who took their place bought equipment in bulk from a big company that was run by strangers, not at the little corner hardware store. Thinking mainly of increasing their bottom line while decreasing their personal workload, they looked for suppliers who could give them the biggest price break, take their credit cards over the phone or Internet, and deliver merchandise to their doors.

But farmers were not the only customers who drifted away from the little store. Town folks either died or moved to other towns. Although Hayward's 249 residents are prosperous by any standards, their lifestyle and shopping habits are different from those of past generations, and the hometown hardware store faces stiff competition. Kids who once rode their bikes to the story to buy Mother's Day candy dishes or spatulas are more likely to wait until they get a ride to Wal Mart. Today's shopper might log on to the Internet and order what he needs from the comfort of home or order from a multitude of catalogs that are delivered to each mailbox day after day.

The transformation of retail business has changed the way most people shop, and most small, locally owned stores eventually throw in the towel. Home Depot came to Albert Lea a few years ago, and in 2003 Super Wal Mart opened its doors a mere six miles west of Leo's Hardware Hank. Those giant stores sit on either side of County Road 46, the road that leads into Hayward. That 12-mile round trip is nothing for today's Hayward residents, and the big box lower prices, modern buildings and greater variety pulled even long-time customers down the road and into those places that are owned by out-of-towners. Hardly anybody knows your name there, and it's hard to find someone to help solve your problems and exchange hometown news.

Hometown news focused on the sale of Leo's Hardware Hank early in 2007. Leo really enjoyed running the store for nearly a quarter century, and he hated to say goodbye, but business had been down and he had passed the age when most people retire. After two years on the market, the store found a new owner. At first it seemed as though he might keep the hardware store open, but now that possibility seems unlikely.

In honor of his retirement, friends and customers crowded into Hayward's Korner Kafe, about fifty yards north of Leo's Hardware Hank, on the afternoon of March 30, 2007, to enjoy a cup of coffee and a piece of cake and to wish Leo well. Some storytelling went on, some reminiscing, and many expressed regrets as they saluted a bygone era. There is not a person alive who can recall a time when that hardware store was not a part of the community of Hayward, but now it seems that the store is destined to become a Minnesota memory.

Leo Aeikens in his hardware store

July 13, 1985: Sisyphus and the Hide-a-Bed
By Joan Claire Graham

During the heat snap of 2006, I heard a newscaster say that the last time Minnesota temperatures rose above 100 degrees was July 13, 1995. After wondering how many people listening could remember exactly what they were doing that day, I phoned my daughters and my Aunt Esther, and we all had fun reminiscing.

We lived in California then, and when my daughter Jennifer graduated from high school in 1993, she began her college studies at Linfield, a small liberal arts school in Oregon. It was a great starter school for a girl whose academic precociousness was offset by her lack of practical experience. With my sister a mere 50 miles away in Salem providing family support, Jennifer left the teeming metropolis of Los Angeles and moved 900 miles north to the sleepy little town of McMinville, Oregon. I hoped that learning to get along in a small town would help her transition from child to adult.

She quickly fit in with the college theater crowd, got her feet on the ground, and started expressing boredom with small-town life. On one of my trips to see a show she was in during her sophomore year, I noticed a flyer on the bulletin board. The Children's Theater Company in Minneapolis was holding auditions for acting interns. Since she was born in Minneapolis, I pointed out the audition notice and encouraged her to give it a shot. Much to my surprise, she followed through, booked a flight to Minneapolis, stayed with friends, and auditioned. A few days later she learned that she had been chosen as one of six interns for the 1995-1996 season at CTC.

Jennifer was supposed to report for duty at the Children's Theater August 1, so she, her sister Susannah and I flew from Los Angeles to Minneapolis the second week in July. That gave her enough time to register for internship credit at the University of Minnesota, find an apartment, furnish the apartment, and settle in before starting her first real job, a 10-month theater internship.

We had great success our first day of apartment hunting and found a nice, big efficiency unit in a nicely restored old building at 18th and

Stevens, immediately available, and within easy walking distance to the theater. We stayed with Aunt Esther in Bloomington and had further good luck finding almost everything Jennifer needed to furnish her apartment on a whirlwind Saturday of garage sales. The only item we were unable to find cheap was a hide-a-bed, which we bought at a store.

Esther's grand nephews, Danan and Ryan, had a truck that they volunteered for moving day, but they could only do it Thursday afternoon. The landlord gave that date thumbs up, and my nephew Christopher joined the crew. All in all, our luck had been great. We had five strong kids, two able-bodied adults, a good-sized truck, and not that much stuff to move. We figured the whole operation would take about an hour, and my cousin Paula invited the whole gang to her condo in Edina for a spaghetti dinner to celebrate the completion of the job. She figured we'd be starving.

Despite our good planning and early success, I knew we were in for a grueling day when I walked outside on moving day, July 13, 1995. The temperature in Death Valley was 119, and in Chicago it was 106. In Minneapolis it was a mere 103, but with high humidity it seemed more like 150. I felt like I was swimming under water—bath water. Health advisories warned people to stay inside, but we had to ignore those warnings because we had a job to do.

The boys arrived with the truck around 4, and we picked up the hide-a-bed at a store a few blocks away. With that loaded on the bottom, we piled the dresser, end tables, lamps, rug, bookshelves, hamper, electric fan, wastebasket, dishes, toaster, microwave, pots and pans, and dinette set on top and headed seventy blocks up Lyndale looking a little bit like the Joads. Esther had the good sense to bring along a cooler filled with drinks, and she, Christopher, Jennifer, Susannah and I followed the truck in her car.

Have I mentioned that the apartment was a third floor walk-up in an old building with very narrow stairways? Our first climb up there went pretty well. The heat and humidity were absolutely stifling, but we felt we were a team with an objective, trying to impress one another with our pluck and mettle, and we were still somewhat refreshed by the air-conditioned car ride. We all grabbed something small, and the effect of adding seven items to an empty apartment was gratifying. I stayed there to put things in their place and turn on the fan, and Esther went downstairs to stay at street level under a shade tree with the cooler full of drinks as the kids bounded down three flights for more stuff. But it was 103 degrees with high humidity, and by the time they arrived upstairs with their second load, their faces were red and streaked with sweat. The small kitchen table and two chairs came in the third load, and a couple of boys carried the dresser while others carried empty drawers. With the bulk of the work finished, everyone chugged a can of pop or two as they eyed the final challenge—the hide-a-bed.

I suggested removing the mattress, thus lightening the load by fifteen or twenty pounds, but in a classic display of teenage hubris, one of the strapping boys said that removing it wouldn't make very much difference, and they might as well just tie a rope around the whole thing, bite the bullet, and begin their climb. Three big boys and two tiny girls should be able to make it. After all, it was only the third floor. By that time we were all swimming in sweat, thinking about our spaghetti dinner, and too hot to argue.

The building's architects back in the early 1900s had maximized rentable living space by minimizing space taken by hallways and stairs. The front staircase was about three and a half feet wide, fully enclosed, with frequent turns, and at the top of each level was a heavy fire door that opened into the stairwell, further reducing space to maneuver. If the stairwell had been a shoe and the hide-a-bed had been a foot, it would have been a perfect fit. There was no wiggle room.

The kids made it up the front stoop and up the first few steps to the main floor. They bit the bullet and began their push to the second floor, but the circular stairway, combined with the size and weight of the hide-a-bed and the narrowness of the space, presented a challenge even for those enterprising and strong kids. With much creative thinking and brute strength, they managed to stand the hide-a-bed on end to get around tight corners. By sheer determination and hard work, they got the thing all the way to the third floor, just shy of the last fire door. The fire door must have been different from the previous ones because, try as they might, they could not get the hide-a-bed through that last door. In fact, it was wedged in the stairwell like a balloon in a teacup, and the tired and sweat-drenched kids could not move it either in or out. Ryan made the pronouncement, "We'll just have to leave it there." And he meant it.

Those who were on the upside of the load took the back stairway down to the street, and those who were on the downside came down the way they had gone up. After tossing down a few more drinks, they held a tribal council. The first thing Jennifer stated, in no uncertain terms, was that the hide-a-bed could not stay lodged in the third floor stairwell. It either had to come in or come out. There must be a fire code to support that fact, she reasoned, and any sane person had to agree. Ryan balked, stating emphatically that it could not be done. The tribe quickly vetoed his vote as the council continued.

Absolutely no outsiders came to their rescue because nobody else was dumb enough to try a Herculean task in that kind of weather. Esther and I were too old to help, and even if we hadn't been, there was no room for more people in the stairwell. The five kids had to figure it out themselves, and tempers wore short as the hot sun bore down. The boys' mother miraculously showed up with more drinks, assessed the progress, and wished everybody luck. By now everyone was drenched to the skin, their hair clinging to their scalps in soggy clumps.

Remember Sisyphus? He was the Greek guy condemned to Hades, where his eternal punishment was pushing a huge rock up a hill, only to be frustrated, time after time, when the rock plummeted back down just before reaching the summit. I thought of Sisyphus– and Hades–that July afternoon that was slowly melting into evening.

After much discussion, the movers decided that their only solution was to marshal their forces to push the hide-a-bed down from the up-side, take it the all the way down the front stairs and start up the back flight of stairs. Since gravity was on their side, they were able to dislodge the thing when the five of them pushed. I felt like crying when I saw it down on the ground where it had started, but I had no remaining body fluids with which to produce tears.

The back stairway of the apartment building was similar in size and shape to the one in front, but it had an open landing on the top floor before the fire door. The kids figured that since they had made their way almost to the third floor hallway via the front stairs, they would be able to succeed in the back because the top floor landing would allow them enough clearance when they opened the last fire door.

I cast another vote for removing the mattress, and to my great astonishment they took my advice. The load became a few pounds lighter, and four kids took the floppy mattress and cushions upstairs while the other re-tied the bed mechanism. Once they were positioned in the back stairway, again the end-over-end method proved to be the only solution for wrapping the hide-a-bed around those tight corners. Even with the lightened and less bulky load, the kids had to stop every few minutes to catch their breath and take drinks. After an hour of struggling, they finally made it through the third floor fire door, and so did the hide-a-bed. They shoved it through the apartment door and fell down on the floor in complete exhaustion. By now it was 7 o'clock.

Everyone was too exhausted to celebrate as we piled into Esther's car and headed for Paula's place to eat our spaghetti supper, but the kids moaned and groaned on the ten-minute ride about how hot and exhausted they were. When we arrived, Susannah and Christopher saw Paula's pool, climbed out of the car and jumped directly into the deep end without conferring or even removing their shoes. I believe this is the only impulsive thing Susannah has ever done in her life.

When they came dripping into Paula's condo, she gave them some big shirts to wear and towels to sit on as she threw their clothes into her dryer. She had no trouble getting rid of all the food she had prepared as the ravenous but re-energized kids conducted a play-by-play of every turn in those stairwells, and we marveled at what their team had accomplished.

It's been many years, but this incident is why my girls, their cousins, my aunt, and I remember exactly what we were doing on July 13, 1995, when the temperature in Minneapolis climbed above one hundred degrees. Jennifer started her Children's Theater internship a couple of weeks later, adapted well to independent living, and lived in that apartment for two years. When she moved out, her dad came to help.

The Stagecoach Opera House in Shakopee
By Tom Butsch

As a University of Minnesota freshman I had only vague ideas of what I wanted to do with my life. I began as a studio art major because I could draw and paint pretty well. I also liked performing in plays, enjoying the community feeling that putting on a show inspired, and along the way, I had picked up the acting bug.

When I got to the U in 1964, I took some art classes and some theater classes, and I have to say the theater classes began to win out. The theater department professors were funny, odd and interesting, while the art teachers were dull and uninspiring. Dr. Arthur Ballet's Introduction to Theater class was like a daily stand-up comedy routine that also provided a thorough grounding in theater history. Some of his lectures had to be closed to keep the hall from overflowing with students curious to see performances like his famous "Ready Kilowatt and the History of Stage Lighting" routine.

The McKnight program that provided graduate students a path to employment at the Guthrie as well as a scholarship ensured a constant supply of talented and experienced actors, directors and designers. This raised the bar for novices, and it made casting for University productions fiercely competitive.

I first got involved in a dormitory drama club and then joined a group mentored by Bob Moulton called Fresh Faces, organized by the theater department to help freshman drama students get their bearings. Moulton was a charismatic, brilliant, former Martha Graham dancer with a Ph.D. who taught stage movement and direction. With a dancer's body, he was a handsome man who was disfigured by two enormous buckteeth that made him look like Lampwick. His teeth, which might have made a lesser personality self-conscious, simply added to his persona. He had a quick, puckish sense of humor, an encyclopedic knowledge of theater history and performance lore, and he devoted considerable time and energy to helping our group dip our toes into the large pool of University theater.

By the end of freshman year, I had actually been cast in two University productions and felt like I was part of the theater community. Then audition notices for the Stagecoach Players went up, and I decided to give it a shot. I had heard about the Stagecoach from my actor friends, and it seemed like a fun way to spend the summer.

Ozzie Klavestad, who owned a restaurant and Western museum between Shakopee and Savage, founded the Stagecoach Opera House of the Bella Union in 1961. Klavestad bore a striking resemblance to Buffalo Bill–especially when he donned his white Western suit and enormous Stetson hat.

To the museum, which housed his enormous and amazing antique gun collection and assortment of vintage music players, Ozzie added an old streetcar barn, which he and his minions transformed into a theater with the help and expertise of Bob Moulton and Wendell Josal, scenic design professor at the U of M. Moulton became the artistic director, and Josal handled the scenery and technical aspects and served as the managing director. Their wives, Elizabeth Josal and Maggie Moulton, handled the ticket office and publicity.

The shows were melodramas and old musicals from the turn of the century, cut down and streamlined to allow plenty of time for the famous Stagecoach olios, musical interludes designed and staged by Moulton. He had an amazing knack, aided and abetted by musical director Vern Sutton, for combining old songs into medleys and mini musicals that were wacky, funny, and even poignant. By 1965, when I auditioned, they had really hit their stride and had arrived at a successful formula that had audiences cheering for the hero, booing and hissing the villain, and shouting for more at curtain call.

For my audition, I arrived at the old Contemporary Dance Studio in Dinkytown, carrying my guitar and trying to control my jangling nerves. The Stagecoach audition was primarily concerned with singing because of the olios. They figured your acting could be improved, but if you couldn't sing or carry a tune, the situation was hopeless. Good singers were highly prized. The company was not very big, and they relied on everyone having good voices.

I already knew Moulton, but auditions are stressful under the best of conditions. Not being a great singer, I faked my way through "The Banks of the Ohio," using a hillbilly accent and playing a country lick on guitar. When I finished, they seemed skeptical, and Vern Sutton asked if I could sing something straight, which I did with somewhat less success. Moulton had me do a monologue that he had heard me do in a Fresh Faces revue that spring. He thought it was hilarious and wanted the others to hear it. That was positive, but not, I feared, enough to make up for my lack of vocal skill. I left feeling I had done okay, but not great.

After a week or so of pins and needles, in the middle of final exams, Wendell Josal called me with the magic words, "Congratulations, you're a Stagecoach Player." There were two categories of player: full company status, which meant you earned $65 a week to play principal roles, and apprentice, who was paid $15 dollars a week to sing in the chorus and play supporting parts.

Everyone worked on costumes and scenery during the day and performed in shows at night. I was offered an even lower category, door apprentice, which meant that when I was not onstage, I would go around to the front and man the door, making sure nobody sneaked into the show. At that point, I didn't care how menial my job was or how low the pay. I was absolutely thrilled to be chosen. Anyone who has ever auditioned knows the ecstatic feeling of getting the part and the despair of being rejected, and I was walking on air that spring, looking forward to an exciting summer in professional theater.

The shows that year were *The Streets of New York*, a melodrama, *Floradora*, a musical from the turn of the century, and *Sherlock Holmes*, the William Gillette version of the detective novels. One Stagecoach policy was that genuine old plays and musicals were performed, as opposed to "mellerdrammers," contemporary plays written to capitalize on the popularity of the old fashioned style. I think this choice came from the academic bent of the artistic staff. Moulton spent time every year at the New York Public Library unearthing old scripts to adapt, and Vern Sutton would come up with esoteric, funny and beautiful songs from the period to use in the olios. Both men were real scholars, and their knowledge and expertise lent credibility to the productions. As college students, we appreciated being able to bring a bit of theatrical history to life.

After much anticipation, we reported to work. We cleaned the theater, started work on the scenery and costumes, attended classes in stage movement and voice taught by Moulton and Sutton, and started rehearsing *The Streets of New York*. The voice and movement classes continued all season and provided a venue to teach new songs and dances as well as a warm up for each night's performance.

Josal heard that I was an art major so he drafted me to help paint backdrops. The Stagecoach had a small stage with limited wing space so scenery was done in the old fashioned "drop and wing" style. We used painted wings and drops that rolled up like window shades to store out of sight in the low ceiling and tall, wooden panels that concealed the backstage areas. A few other pieces and furniture completed the settings.

I had fun painting backdrops on the paint frame under a shed roof at the back of the theater. While building and painting, we rehearsed the upcoming show and olios. We worked long days, and once the shows began, we routinely worked 12 to 14-hour days with only the occasional day off. In the first show, I played a poor old man, Mr. Puffy, whose family was exploited and reduced to poverty by the evil banker, Gideon Bloodgood, played with mustache twirling malevolence by Vern Sutton. I was in a couple of olios and spent time watching the door and working on my soft shoe and time step, which Moulton was teaching us during our physical and vocal warmups.

It was tremendous fun. We became a big family, involved in all aspects of each other's lives with friendships and romances, hanging out, parties, and a lot of hard work. After the first show, I was promoted to regular apprentice. I was either doing something right or my promotion could have occurred because Willie Lauder, another apprentice, broke his leg while running down the aisle during the big fire sequence in *Streets of New York*. I'd rather think it was due to my talent, but I can't be sure.

Someone else was hired as door apprentice, and I spent all my time working on scenery and performing in shows. I got a better part in *Floradora,* and I also got to do the opening number, a rollicking tune with a pounding piano vamp, guns firing to wake up the audience, and the girls exiting with a fold-out stagecoach. This number traditionally followed Ozzie's quirky curtain speech, in which he welcomed the audience and invited them to cheer for our "actors and actoreens" and hiss and boo the villains. He cut quite a figure in his full Buffalo Bill regalia and always got a great response.

Floradora is a musical comedy with a unique structure. Act I takes place in Ireland with wealthy aristocrats and an itinerant phrenologist (practitioner who makes diagnoses based on the study of bumps on a patient's head). The action moved to a Hawaiian perfumery for the second act, complete with grass skirts and leis. The original *Floradora* sextet, in the 1890s, featured six Broadway beauties who became the toast of the town and all married millionaires, according to legend.

I played one of the guys in the Coach's version of "Tell Me Pretty Maiden," the sextet's show-stopping number that had them standing in the aisles in Victorian New York. Men wore tails, and girls twirled and posed in frilly pink dresses and parasols. The finale was a silly Hawaiian war chant with the girls misting the audience with large perfume atomizers. All shows ended with Woody Guthrie's "So Long, it's Been Good to Know You." We all ran around to the front of the theater and lined up to say goodnight and thank the audience for coming, a Stagecoach tradition.

One unique thing about the Stagecoach was that they served beer and setups at the Western bar at the back of the theater. Setups meant you brought your own booze, and the bartender provided the mix. This made for some raucous audiences who were encouraged to hiss and boo and shout comments. On Friday and Saturday nights, when the second show audience had time to get well lubricated, things could really get loud.

One night at *Floradora* there was a particularly obnoxious guy in the front row who was many sheets to the wind when the show started and got more loaded as the night went on. He thought his incoherent ad-libs were hilarious, and he reached out to paw the girls whenever they got out on the runway around the piano pit. The ladies planned revenge, however, and executed it flawlessly. During the finale, instead of pointing their perfume atomizers up to gently waft scent over the audience, they trained their weapons on the drunken lout in front and thoroughly saturated him. Generally, though, we loved those weekend audiences and they loved the shows. It was impossible to feel tired or give a bad performance with those energetic crowds carrying you along.

As the season wore on, I found I enjoyed working on scenery more and more. I would arrive early and work on my days off to help Bill Rowe, the scene designer, paint drops or build and paint scenery. As we approached the opening of each show, Bill and I would work longer hours as the deadline approached. I was also rehearsing the new show. Changeovers were fast to reduce financially unprofitable down time so cast and crew sacrificed sleep.

The last show that season, my first of three Stagecoach summers, was *Sherlock Holmes*. As a scrawny teenager, I was horribly miscast as Dr. Watson, but I did my best and audiences seemed to accept me. I had a featured part in the graduation olio, giving an impassioned speech from an old graduation manual that Moulton had unearthed. "We who stand tonight at the meeting between a happy past and an unknown future, etc." The rest of the olio was an inspired send-up of old fashioned graduation ceremonies, complete with all the obscure lyrics to "Land of Hope and Glory," better known as "Pomp and Circumstance." The other highlight was the first act finale, the Oriental olio, which featured belly dancers, snake charmers, chorus boys in giant red pantaloons and fezzes, and girls in veils and harem pants.

This olio featured one of the funniest musical numbers I have ever seen. The Turkish chorus entered down the aisles, which meant that we had to run bare chested outside from our dressing room to the door by the bar, a cold excursion in Minnesota October. I really came to appreciate its staging because I saw it every night from the back of the house. "Pale Hands" was an operatic duet featuring tenor Vern Sutton as a sheik and Sharon Rhome, the company's diva soprano, as an Arabian temptress. The two were seated on a bench, and as Vern sang beautifully of "Pale Hands I love, beside the Shalimar," Sharon lovingly caressed him. Soon, however, Sharon's hands became increasingly active, fondling Vern, stroking his hair, his clothes and generally becoming a distraction. Vern, increasingly annoyed, attempted to contain her hands, only to have them break free, again and again. Finally, he got both her hands under control.

Glowing with triumph, he plunged back into the song. But now, miraculously, another arm appeared to stroke his face and then another began to fondle his chest. Looking confused, he released Sharon's hands to deal with the new threat, and she immediately launched another digital assault of her own. Now, as the song continued, Vern resembled a man dealing with a swarm of writhing pit vipers as he tried valiantly to finish the song and remove the invading hands. By this time, the audience was howling with laughter. For as long as I have worked in the theater, I don't believe I have heard that volume of laughter equaled.

As the song finished, the hand situation miraculously returned to normal and Vern leapt to his feet, looked around wildly for the source of his woes, and finding nothing, rushed off leaving Sharon sitting innocently on the bench. The secret, of course, was slender Kathy Holmay with her long arms, concealed behind the tiny bench, adding two extra limbs to the mayhem. It was an example of how a simple trick could turn a silly old song into a comic masterpiece in the hands of a brilliant director and some great comic performers.

The season slowed down in autumn, and we went from performing eight shows a week to just a few on weekends. After the last performance, we buttoned up the theater for winter, had a wrap party, and went back to school. We kept in contact during the year, and many came back the next summer. Subsequent seasons featured George M. Cohan's *45 Minutes from Broadway, Around the World in Eighty Days, The Geisha, and The Count of Monte Cristo.*

Many Stagecoach Players went on to theater and film careers. Vern Sutton became head of the University music department, sang with the Minnesota Opera, and became a familiar voice to radio listeners on A *Prairie Home Companion.* Cloyce Morrow had a nice run of success in feature films and national commercials, and her brother Barry, who was an apprentice during the 1966 season, won an Oscar for his screenplay, *Rain Man.* Kay Dengel starred in the San Francisco Company of *You're a Good Man Charlie Brown* and made a good living doing voice overs. Ivar Brogger acted for many years at the Guthrie and has had a nice career in film, stage and TV. Others became college professors and teachers. My friend Bill Macklin married Paige Hatfield, one of our "actoreens." She taught music in Richfield and Lakeville, and he became an attorney, State Representative and judge. Who could have imagined that?

Audiences enjoyed entertainment at The Stagecoach Opera House for eighteen years, but times and tastes change over time. After presenting

1,898 performances of 44 shows to 300,000 patrons, management brought down the final curtain and closed the doors for good in 1979.

After three Stagecoach seasons I gave up acting, and, encouraged by Josal, Moulton, and others, became a scenic designer. I worked at Chanhassen Dinner Theater for many years, freelanced, did Hollywood sitcoms, and for the past 20 years have been an art director at Disneyland. I have done shows at Radio City Music Hall, in Tokyo, Las Vegas, Florida Seattle, Arizona and California, but I have never had as much fun and satisfaction in the theater as I had during that first season at the Coach. I'm sure the experiences I had and the people I met played a pivotal role in the direction my life took. The Stagecoach pointed me toward a life in the theater, and those long summer days of work and nights of performing gave me a taste of how much fun it could be to work hard at a job you love. And I've been lucky enough to be able to do just that.

Los Angeles resident Tom Butsch designs events and shows at Disneyland.

Paige Hatfield Macklin, Tom Butsch, Mac Reynolds, Scott Johnson and Vern Sutton perform "Pet Names" by George M. Cohan at the Stagecoach Opera House in Shakopee, 1966.

Mabel for Strongest Woman
By Kathryn L. Nelson

To Garrison Keillor, after the annual street dance during which there was no Strongest Woman Contest, I feel a need to apologize to you for the unruly Nelson family who showed up at your dance advocating Mabel for Strongest Woman. I was shamelessly pushy, a characteristic not much valued in our Swedish Lutheran family. Perhaps it's because I married a Kuwaiti, and we have a son with Down syndrome – I've been catapulted into a subculture where people ask for and even demand what they think they need, whether it's an armed invasion or a good education.

But here's the thing: Mabel really is the strongest woman, but she is 84 years old and some of her children are fast approaching 60, and it was really hard to get them together in the first place – not your problem, I know – but they would only come to a street dance if they thought their mother would be entering the Strongest Woman Contest, which, it turned out, didn't take place.

So, we made buttons and signs to impress the boy siblings (actually, that was the idea of friends who would like to be adopted by Mabel and thought it would help their chances). But really, she was embarrassed, and she was glad there was no contest because while it was nice to have her children all show up and wear silly buttons and huddle under a sign with a picture of young Mabel and her prize-winning heifer, the great thing, she said, was that she didn't have to stand up and make a fool of herself.

Did I mention t-shirts? That was granddaughter Melissa's idea, t-shirts for the next generation, which she made at Kinko's. And then the woman who got us started thinking about entering the contest showed up – she's the one who won the contest last year because she raised a pot-bellied pig, and Mabel said very softly, "I raised a 1000-pound heifer."

So, lest I digress, here is Mabel for you. She contracted smallpox at birth from her mother, and the doctor didn't bother with a birth certificate because she shouldn't have lived through it, but she did, which explains why her celebrated birthday never matched her birth certificate.

At age 6 she drove the pickup (standing up) down the rows of the field near Osseo while her dad and brothers pitched potatoes into the back. By high school she was throwing the potato sacks herself, all the while learning to play the tuba and a mean shortstop and reading every book in the school library. It was about this time that the heifer came into the picture – a 4-H project that won her first place at the State Fair and the right to contribute her winnings to the family pot.

She eventually became a school nurse and married a Navy veteran who was very fun and also an alcoholic, and when things got bad, she worked the late shift at Hennepin General Hospital, took the bus to the end of the line, and hoped he would pick her up to go back to the 15-foot trailer where they lived with kid one and kid two. Then Dad got the mumps and shouldn't have been able to, but managed to father kids three and four. Somewhere in between those two she put her foot down, he joined Alcoholics Anonymous, and for the rest of his life she went with him every Tuesday and every Friday to AA meetings, missing the Santa Lucia contest at church for the love of him.

I could go on and on, which I see I have already done, but I just wanted to explain why my son pressed a button into your hand and why we hung around in tight little knots waiting to see if there might be a surprise Strongest Woman Contest after all. We received our just reward for being so forward, by the way; we missed the meatloaf dinner.

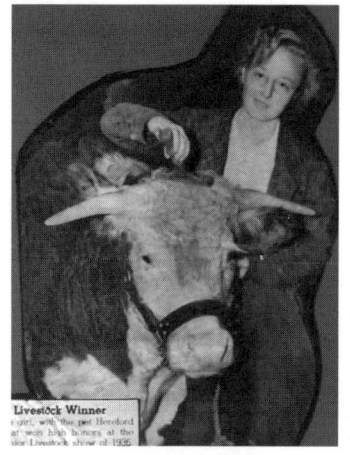

Young Mabel

Actually, Mabel doesn't really like meatloaf; she just wanted to stay around and dance, even though the rest of the family was getting pretty tired. In fact, the boys didn't make it past the mid-point of the evening, but that's boys for you. No offense, I know you're a boy, but you've always made it to the end of the dance. It's just that in my family the women are so much stronger.

P.S. We've taken the liberty of saying, "Mabel *is* the Strongest Woman, no contest."

Minneapolis resident Kathryn L. Nelson wrote the novel, **Pemberley Manor**. *Dividing her writing time between Minnesota and Kuwait, she enjoys people.*

Daniel Gainey, A Minnesotan Who Affected My Life
By Kathy A. Megyeri

Just as Minnesota's favorite sons Charles Lindberg and Hubert Humphrey affected so many lives, tycoon and philanthropist Daniel C. Gainey of Josten's Manufacturing fame personally affected mine. His rags to riches story truly exemplifies the American dream.

In 1897, Otto Josten opened a small jewelry and watch repair shop in Owatonna. That same year, Daniel C. Gainey was born on a dilapidated farm near Lewiston. In 1906, Josten began producing class rings, and after Otto Josten's death in 1936, Gainey expanded the business and eventually became the majority owner. Gainey had many interests and maintained his positive attitude by creating things, perfecting them, and moving on to other projects. Common sense was more important than smarts, he always said, so he loved to tell stories and give his opinions on Minnesota's political scene. He was never shy about expressing his feelings and used to conclude his anecdotes by saying, "The best advice is to carefully follow the Ten Commandments, but do that with some reservation. Making people happy would be another good tenant to follow, but that can lead to soft-headedness. If fifty percent are do-gooders for the other fifty percent, that can ruin a country."

Shortly after his birth, the Gainey family moved to Bemidji, a rough town of 5,000 people and fifty saloons. Dan started school in third grade because his mother said he was as big as the boys of that age, but that proved to be a handicap because he hadn't learned the alphabet. However, by the time he graduated from high school, he was the top scholar in his class.

He started working as a child, first polishing shoes and then helping a baker. He told of showing up for work at 5 a.m. in his bare feet and sitting on the wood pile until the boss unlocked the door to let him in. Dan played football and basketball in high school while working long hours. He received a $100 scholarship to Hamline University in St. Paul but didn't decide to attend until the day before classes began. His father told him they could get along without his $1.75 a week paycheck so he decided at the last minute to go, although he told his family that if they needed him, he'd return home.

He received a BA degree in 1921 and then coached for a year at Hancock High School. The next summer he sold insurance, but a friend told him that Bob Josten, son of Otto, had heard of him and wanted a young fellow with "punch" to help him improve his Owatonna jewelry business. Dan agreed to talk with him.

Otto and Bob Josten interviewed Dan and told him that they had been in business 25 years and had little to show for it. Therefore, they could only pay Dan $100 a month if he would come on board. Dan consented because he appreciated their integrity and fine craftsmanship. The Jostens decided to sell the watch repair part of their business to focus on manufacturing class rings and challenged Gainey to see "what you can do with that part of the business." Dan was enthralled with the idea of manufacturing but wanted part ownership in the business. He offered to buy enough shares so that he would have 53% of Jostens, but assured both men he would not leave and convinced both Jostens that if such an arrangement worked, they would succeed as a team. The Jostens told Dan that he did not need to pay cash for the stock because they knew he was a careful, thrifty man. Dan told them, "If I can make this thing a success, all of us are going to be fine. If I can't, we'll go broke." The Jostens agreed.

Each year the company made more money as graduates bought rings that were reasonably priced and of good quality. In 1945, the company expanded their product line to include announcements, and in 1950, they added yearbooks. Dan's directive to the company was to deliver yearbooks on time and to take orders only from schools that were dissatisfied with their present companies. He pulled together some of the best designers, die cutters and sales crew in the industry. Gainey made it a point to hire well-groomed, handsome and attractive men for his sales staff and positioned them in high school cafeterias to show their product lines. He instituted many innovations while heading the company and influenced customers' buying habits by offering small sized rings for women, personalized school insignias, and multi-colored stones. He served as president of the company from 1933-1959 and then as chairman of the board emeritus and head of the operations committee.

During his presidency, Gainey approached my father, Sid Wilker, who ran a successful Pure Oil station and garage on the main street of

Owatonna. Gainey needed a clean, modern, reasonably priced motel where his salesmen could stay when they came to town for training and sales seminars. My father agreed, and within a year, he opened the Modern Aire on Highway 14 in Owatonna. My parents hired an architect who designed the motel so that customers' cars could be parked next to their rooms, which allowed salesmen to unload their sample cases each evening and rearrange their displays of rings, announcements and yearbooks. Such a convenience was revolutionary at that time because downtown hotels with adjacent parking lots and stairs to climb were still the mainstay of the hospitality industry.

Both my parents maintained the rooms, opened a small coffee shop on site, and made the young Josten's sales staff feel at home; after all, Gainey himself had commissioned the place. Some years later, when the freeway was built around Owatonna, my father converted the Modern Aire into small rental units for those who desired longer stays in town. He then opened the Country Hearth Motel adjacent to I35, but it still served, to a large degree, Josten's sales personnel. The men enjoyed my mother's home-baked chocolate chip cookies each evening, and for years, she followed their personal lives as they spoke to her of children born and wed, wives left at home, and grandchildren arriving. The years of the traveling salesmen in the 1950s, '60s and early '70s provided a stable income for my parents.

Meanwhile, Dan Gainey's only son, Daniel J., was practically born at the company. Gainey Sr. became Chairman of the Board of Directors and moved to Santa Barbara, California. He and his son purchased a ranch there because Daniel C. had developed a growing passion for breeding Arabian horses. His love for these horses had begun in 1940 when he was given his first Arabian horse by some of his salesmen. He carefully bred them and developed a strain of Arabians that were different from the other kinds bred in America at that time. His particular strain had stronger legs with longer, finer necks. Gainey, who once gave two of these horses to President Dwight D. Eisenhower, was a governing member of the Arabian Horse Registry from 1942-73, including a 14-year term as president from 1958-73. He also became a director and officer of many business associations, was a trustee of Hamline University, a member of the Board of Regents of the University of Minnesota, and national treasurer of the Republican Party during Eisenhower's administration.

Gainey built a palatial estate in Owatonna. St. Paul architect Edwin Lundie designed a French-Norman style mansion that took five years to construct. It featured padded silk brocade walls, marble throughout the home, parquet floors, gold fixtures, and a Waterford crystal chandelier, remarkable in its day. Still, Gainey disliked cold weather and enjoyed going south for the winters. He used his drives across country to sell rings and announcements and to hire men to develop more business in the Southern states. Outside Scottsdale, Arizona, he and his wife purchased a 700-acre winter home, but he also enjoyed the Gainey horse ranch in California. As Dan aged, his Mayo Clinic doctors advised him to work less, but to him, that was impossible. He said, "I get up at six in the morning and I'm busy all day until I go to sleep about nine at night. I have no fear of death as long as it is comfortable. I have had a great life because I have had the pleasure of doing good for others. I have loved and been loved, hated and been hated, but above all, I have lived."

When Dan died at age 81 in 1979, the Gainey property in Owatonna was bequeathed to the University of St. Thomas in St. Paul. Ground was broken in 1981 for a conference center building that was constructed adjacent to the Gainey home, and the stallion barn was converted into classrooms for St. Thomas graduate programs, meetings, and classes.

In 2007, Josten's celebrates its 110th anniversary. It evolved from a small jewelry business in rural Minnesota to the nation's leader in all categories of school commemorative products. It became a major innovator in casting stone settings and engraving. My uncle, Clarence Kriesel, was employed his entire career as a master engraver at Josten's, and my husband still wears the belt buckle Kriesel crafted for him in 1966. Gainey was especially good to his long-time employees. After 25 years of service, Gainey presented my uncle with the customary gold watch, and my aunt received sterling silver tableware (place settings for twelve) at an elaborate dinner held to honor long-serving employees.

Josten's has made over fifty million class rings and all six NBA championship rings for the Chicago Bulls. Its product line includes medals and trophies for professional, college, and high school athletes as well as for Olympic and Special Olympic games. It has produced nearly two hundred million yearbooks and provides more than half the schools in the U.S. with graduation announcements, certificates, diplomas, caps and gowns, and other commemoratives. Josten's Photography leads the digital revolution in producing school portraits and graduation photos.

Ten years ago Josten's Renaissance began a structured program of recognition and incentive opportunities for students and teachers. More than 300 schools now embrace this program called Pride and Spirit. Renaissance is the only privately-sponsored program of its kind in America. Their GIVE program supports scholarships, service organizations, civic groups and the arts. Since 1976, the Josten's foundation has contributed over twenty-five million dollars to cultural and educational projects nationwide. Josten's International has brought employment to subsidiaries in Latin and South America, Asia and Europe.

My association with Gainey's legacy is twofold. I still wear my Owatonna high school class ring (1961) made by Josten's. Last September, I attended a writers' convention in Scottsdale at the Gainey Ranch. In 1980, Daniel J. Gainey sold all but 80 acres of the Arabian horse ranch to be transformed to a world-class destination featuring a Hyatt Resort Hotel. This 620-acre second home of his father's became one of the premier convention and resort facilities in the nation. Its spectacular 27-acre golf course, breath-taking view of the surrounding mountains and up-scale amenities like paved walking and biking trails and outstanding restaurants continue the Gainey legacy of quality and service.

In 1995, Gainey sold the remaining 80 acres of his ranch to developers who created the lavish Gainey Suites Hotel, which hosts one of the finest spas in the nation. When I wandered into the clubhouse for lunch last fall, I spotted a brass plaque on the wall that paid homage to Josten's founder Daniel C. Gainey and his favorite Arabian stallion that was bred on that ranch. My parents retired from the motel industry that Dan encouraged them to start, but in Arizona the Gainey family offers one of the finest facilities in the hospitality industry. The irony is that a fellow Minnesotan like Daniel C. Gainey continues to touch my life in unexpected ways and in faraway places. What a tribute to the entrepreneurial spirit, genius, and generosity of a fellow Minnesotan that Owatonna still calls its own.

*Owatonna native Kathy Megyeri is a former English teacher who has contributed to all seven **Minnesota Memories** books and to the **Chicken Soup** series. She lives in Washington, DC and can be reached at Megyeri@Juno.com.*

How I Became a Recycler
By Steve Swanson

I was a fourth grader at the Minnetonka Mills grade school in 1942. Olive drab trucks and tanks that rolled by on railroad flatcars behind our school reminded us daily that a war we scarcely understood was going on somewhere in the world. Our other reminder that spring was the first of many scrap drives our school organized to help the war effort.

Our wartime enemies early on controlled much of the world's bauxite (aluminum) and most of the world's rubber plantations. Recycling, therefore, became an important part of the war effort, and kids willingly pitched in to help. We collected paper, brass, iron, copper, aluminum and rubber.

Posters helped mobilize recycling efforts during World War II.

Because rain would damage them, we kept all the newspapers and magazines stored inside, but we piled metal and rubber into small mountains behind the hog-wire fence on our schoolyard. I hooked my

Radio Flyer red wagon behind my Silver King bike (how much would that be worth today?), and Bruce Tiffany and I scoured our rural neighborhood door-to-door. Mr. Fletcher had gone out of chicken ranching and gave us some feed and watering pans. Mrs. Van Guilder gave us a hot water bottle, a hose and several corks made of rubber, along with (oh, the embarrassment) two girdles.

Those small contributions helped our recycling pile grow taller. And then came my "coup de ferrous"–a buried tractor. The previous summer, our neighbor across the road, Tom Huus, had shown me a Case tractor out by his shed, three-fourths buried. "I got mad one day," he said, "and just buried it."

I told our teacher about Tom's buried tractor. Boy, was she excited! "We'll bring our shovels from home," she announced to our wide-eyed class as she shook her finger in Hitler's direction, "and dig it out ourselves." This seemed like a real possibility.

But it turned out to be a joke. Tom had only buried the tin hood, the tin fenders and the steering wheel shaft. It *looked* like a buried tractor. We won the war, partly with our mountains of scrap, and some of us became lifetime recyclers. Jokers like Tom Huus are hard to find today. Too bad.

Steve Swanson is a retired Lutheran minister and St. Olaf English professor living in Northfield. This childhood experience inspired his four-volume set of **Earthkeeper Mysteries***, chapter books for young readers.*

Taking Care of Shetland Ponies
By Elizabeth Scott (James) Stoesz

When I was growing up near Elko in the 1920s, we received the Minneapolis newspaper every day, but it was always a day late because it was mailed from Minneapolis. Dad liked the world news and farm news, and Mother enjoyed those, along with the women's page. We kids read the funnies.

While reading the ads one September day, Dad saw one that grabbed his attention. A man who earned his living by giving pony rides to children at fairs and recreation areas wanted someone to board ponies for the winter. I think Dad always liked horses because I have a 1909 picture of him on their South Dakota claim with a number of horses he was raising. Dad called the man who ran the ad, and they made a deal for us to take two ponies, Brownie and Buster. The second year we added Queen so we had three.

We rode them all over the area and even learned to stand up on their backs and do trick riding. Brownie was so small that my brothers could stand on the ground and straddle him. He could ride in the car behind the front seat, and he would even come into the house. He was very well coordinated and could stand on his hind legs and walk toward us. We would ride the ponies to Elko, Hazelwood and Isvold, and out to the pasture to herd our cows.

In the winter we rode them to school, and we'd tie up the reins and send the ponies home. They sometimes stopped along the way to dig away the snow and eat whatever was underneath. Then Dad would get a call from an angry neighbor, and he would have to go out somewhere and bring the ponies home.

Those ponies were great entertainment for us kids. One of us would ride and hold a rope while another on skis or a sled was pulled along on the snow. But they had a practical purpose too. We used the ponies to drive the cattle to the creek for a drink.

One day Dad received a milk check for $500, a lot of money in those days, and it still is to me. He gave my sister Sue and me the check and told us to take it to the Elko bank. We rode to town and deposited the check, and the next day the bank closed for good and Dad never received the $500 check back. That was the beginning of the Great Depression, and many people lost their money that way.

For three years we took care of the ponies from September after the State Fair until just before Memorial Day. It was great fun for us, and good training for what came next. Our neighbor, who had purchased a bronco, turned him out to pasture and couldn't catch him. He raffled the horse off for 25 cents a ticket, and Dad won. He caught and trained the bronco, and we kids rode bareback until we acquired a saddle.

Even though we lived on a farm and had to do a lot of work, we still had time for fun. Taking care of those ponies is one of my fond memories of those good times.

A Shetland pony that was placed on a farm after Labor Day

Elizabeth Scott (James) Stoesz, graduated from Faribault High School in 1937. She lived in Prescott, Arizona and died shortly after submitting this story.

The Big Storm of April 1997
By Muriel (Vernon) Johnson

I don't even have to exaggerate to impress my grandchildren with this story about a terrible storm that affected us for an entire week in 1997. That's how bad it was. We had gone to Karlstad the afternoon of Friday, April 4, and Vernon had bought a two-wheel trailer to pull behind the tractor he uses for yard work. It wasn't raining, but after we got home we began to notice raindrops on the windows. That was what they had forecasted so we went to bed that night with no worries and slept well.

We woke up Saturday morning to find our steps covered with ice. I didn't dare step outside. It was drizzling, but the temperature was cold enough so that trees, wires and everything else sparked with ice. A strong northwest wind added to the chill. We did our usual Saturday housework, and Vernon made his "shipwreck hot dish" for lunch. After washing the dishes I decided to wash my hair before sitting down to rest. I had just settled down around 2:15 when "Bingo!" out went the lights.

Going without lights is bad enough, but when the electric thermostat goes out, so does the heat. We had a little kerosene heater in the attic, which we thought would help us out for a while, so Vernon brought that down. When we looked at the fuel gauge, we were disappointed to see that the tank was only half full. With no way to get more we decided to burn it sparingly and make it last as long as possible. We lit our little heater in the kitchen and put a blanket over the doorway to help keep the heat in the kitchen. The top of the heater was warm enough to boil water for coffee and reheat leftover hot dish for supper, so that first day went well. We turned off the heater and crawled under the bedcovers and slept well.

We woke up Sunday to a cold house and a blizzard raging outside, driven by that strong northwest wind. We had gotten about ten inches of snow, and it was blowing and drifting. All church and other town activities were cancelled and everything was at a standstill. Northwest Minnesota was in trouble because all towns and farms in Kittson County were without power. We did have phone service, so we checked on one another and tried to keep our spirits up. Our driveway was blocked so we couldn't go anywhere.

As nightfall approached we had to decide what to do with the small amount of fuel left in the heater. Our upstairs would be too cold for sleeping and so would our living room couch so we closed off everything but the kitchen. We didn't have room there for a bed so we dragged the recliners in there and went up in the attic to find the sleeping bags. I crawled into mine wearing two pairs of sweat pants, two sweat shirts, socks, booties, cap and gloves, and it wasn't too bad.

Wearing insulated coveralls, sweatshirt, sweat pants, slippers, cap and gloves, Vernon lit the stove to warm the kitchen before we went to sleep. When it got toasty he turned off the heater and hopped into his sleeping bag on the recliner. We slept fast and hard until about 2 a.m., when we woke up in the cold. We felt we'd better not light the heater yet so we huddled down and tried to sleep a little longer. At 6 a.m. Vernon decided to light the heater and let it burn until there was no more fuel. It was now Monday, April 7.

We heated water for coffee and filled two thermos bottles with hot water. By 9 o'clock we ran out of fuel, and there was no way we could get more. Now what? Arnold Hilde called and offered to plow our driveway, so that was good. Shortly later, Avis called from the nursing home in Karlstad. She had stayed there overnight and said we should come. Bonnie, the supervisor, said there would be room—surely an answer to our prayers.

We didn't waste any time changing into clean clothes. Taking our sleeping bags and pillows, we started driving to Karlstad. We got as far as Marvin Mattson's and the road was blocked, so Vernon backed up to the mile line and took the road past East Emmaus Church and turned on the tar road into Karlstad.

Vernon and I were given a double mattress on the floor of the conference room. We put our sleeping bags on top of the mattress, and they gave us sheets and a blanket. How warm it was! We, along with several other storm guests, were treated royally with food and the comforts of home. After the evening meal, we all sat around and shared stories and jokes, forgetting about the weather.

We did not have hot water, and we had to use the cold sparingly because the Karlstad water tower was draining and there was no electricity to pump it full again. Bonnie found someone who had water, and got a couple young fellows to haul it over in several big plastic buckets. After supper they flushed all the toilets by dumping water into them.

Our jam session adjourned around 10 p.m. and everyone headed for our various sleeping quarters. Vernon and I had the conference room to ourselves and were very comfortable and cozy. Around 2 a.m. we woke up and saw the streetlight shining in our window. Karlstad had gotten current!

When we woke up around 7, we could hear workers up and busy. It was a sunny day and around 4 degrees above zero. The main topic of conversation in the employees' dining room during breakfast was concern about whether pipes had frozen or if sump holes had overflowed in basements because there was no power to start the pumps. After breakfast Vernon took Avis home to check, and her pipes and everything were okay. Lawrence Anderson's furnace was fine, but his pipes were broken so Vernon called the city office and Solland Plumbing.

On our way home we stopped at Ruth's because she had some kerosene left. Now that the current was on in Karlstad, she could use her furnace. There was no current on at home when we arrived, but all was well with the pipes and the basement. Vernon filled the kerosene heater and warmed up the kitchen. Our friend Ron brought us two more cans of kerosene so we now had enough to last a while, and another friend, Debbie, sent us hot supper, which tasted great. Around 5:30 Wayne Jacobson brought us a small generator and hooked it up so we could run our furnace. It had a small fuel tank and could only run about an hour before the tank had to be refilled. Vernon turned it off when we went to sleep, but we were able to sleep upstairs in our own bed.

Vernon got up early Wednesday, April 9, and tried to start the generator, but it wouldn't go. Wayne had said it was hard to start, and we had to get help. It was only 40 degrees inside, and 4 degrees outside, sunny and cold. A friend called and invited us to their place to shower, shave, and fix my hair. They had a generator hooked on to a tractor so they had water, lights and heat. We hadn't showered since Friday so we happily took them up on their offer. We drove in to Kennedy and learned that they were serving dinner at the community center so we went there and enjoyed the company of others affected by the storm.

After dinner, we drove to Karlstad, east of Kennedy. The R.E.A. poles made a broken mess on the ground, with electric wires twisted all over the fields. We had heard that Wikstrom's store had gotten a load of generators, but when we got there, they were all gone. We decided that our hard-to-start-one-hour generator was better than nothing, but later Brian called to say they found one, and he and Corey Wikstrom came out and hooked up a 4,000-watt generator with an electric starter to the furnace. They also hooked up an electric cord to the generator, which allowed us to run one appliance at a time and keep a lamp lit. This helped us heat our food and stay comfortable, and the furnace ran all night.

By Thursday we were functioning pretty well with our generator, and Vernon drove around and checked on a few neighbors. We had a few phone calls, including one from Seattle, where our northwestern Minnesota weather had made the news.

On Friday we drove to Kennedy and saw that they were unloading new poles where the old ones were lying on the ground. We went to Hallock and had a hamburger for lunch, and then back to Kennedy, where we saw new poles standing and wire being stretched. That evening we drove to Heritage School in Karlstad for their appreciation banquet, and when coming home we noticed some yard lights on. Could it really be?

Sure enough, our yard light was on. We turned off the generator and hooked up the electrical plug in the panel that gave us our furnace, lights and appliances. We called everyone to let them know we were back in business after an unforgettable week. Brian came out the next day and got the generator, which we appreciated. We thanked God and our friends and neighbors for helping to keep us safe throughout the whole ordeal.

Muriel Johnson is a retired schoolteacher. She and Vernon, who have been married sixty years, live in Lake Bronson during warm weather and St. Louis Park during the winter.

Transportation and Commerce
By Richard Hall

Around the time I was born, it was said that there were only a few thousand miles of paved roads in America, and most of those were located near major cities, especially in the East. Roads in small towns and rural areas were poorly engineered, impassable at times, and poorly marked. With the invention of the Ford Model T and rapid increase of automobiles, the web of roads grew from town to town, and the demand for better roads from state to state grew like wildfire. Highway 218 near Austin became a two-lane cement thoroughfare all the way to the Twin Cities.

When they laid Highway 218 on the north edge of Austin, several crews camped in large tents across from the Oakwood Cemetery, and their equipment was stored there too. Equipment was different then, as they did hand labor using picks and shovels.

It's hard to realize with our super highways and ramps today that we thought our very narrow two-lane cement highways with the rolled edge or curb on the side were so wonderful. Traffic wasn't nearly as heavy as today because not many people had cars. Yet, there were many accidents because of the kinds of cars and roads. Roads were narrow and often without a shoulder, there were no signs to warn people of curves or bumps, there were no seat belts, tires were undependable, many cars had open tops or tops made of fabric, and when you signaled you had to roll down the window and stick your hand out. When someone got killed in an automobile accident, they would put up a little marker sign. Some curves or crossings had several markers from fatal accidents.

The highway or main road always ran through the main street of every town, because this was the business hub of the city where the restaurants, stores and hotels were located. With better roads came the popularity of bus transportation. The Jefferson and Greyhound were two of Austin's early bus lines, and passengers could make connections going any direction. At times, the buses going in and out of Austin were so full of people that there was standing room only. Men were expected to stand and let the women have the seats. Most of the luggage and some freight were carried on a rack on top of the bus.

Entering town, passengers moved to the front of the bus and told the driver which corner to drop them off at. I remember coming back at night and seeing a number of people getting off at corners and walking home in the dark, carrying suitcases, bags or boxes. The rest of us got off at the Fox Hotel.

The Fox Hotel was Austin's largest hotel and also a bus stop. Sometimes its large porches, lobbies and sidewalks were overcrowded with people who were either waiting to get on the bus or seeing someone off. Passengers could also purchase tickets at the hotel.

The Fox Hotel in Austin

Until after World War II, when prosperity brought more autos and buses, Austin was kind of a divided town. It wasn't intended to be a class society, but there were a number of contributing factors. Much of the town character was deeply rooted in the early social structure, where the leadership came from business and professional town fathers. There may have been a few exceptions, but when you worked for someone you had to be careful about what you said because you might lose your job. When Roosevelt ran against Hoover for president, some employers told their employees that they wanted them to vote for Hoover.

Some of Austin's families had prospered over the years, and their wealth showed in their large homes, mostly located north and west of Main Street and north on Lansing Avenue. People who could afford it tried to live within walking distance of businesses, church and the high school. This made life easier.

A few large homes were scattered around the west side. Although most have been remodeled, you can still tell the period in which they were built. Most were framed and painted white. Some had green or black trim, which was popular, and there were a few cream and gray houses. They had large porches on the front or side and a porch or shed behind the house and a barn in the back. There was enough land to keep a horse for transportation, a cow, a few chickens, and those with children often had a pony. And of course, everybody had a garden, some apple trees or a berry patch.

Main Street was the center of Austin's businesses in the 1930s and also a social hub. The big event of the week was payday on Friday or Saturday. Stores closed at 5 during the week when the storekeepers went home for supper. On Sunday a few gas stations were open, and one or two neighborhood grocery stores opened for an hour or two in the afternoon. Otherwise, commerce came to a halt.

Saturday night was a big night in the little town. In the summer you could see families walking for blocks to shop uptown. Sometimes they would be pulling a wagon to haul groceries.

Those with an automobile would take the family and maybe a neighbor along. Farmers would fill their cars, or if they had a truck you might see kids riding in the box. They all wanted to take advantage of Saturday sales.

There were only three stoplights on Main Street, and I think they were the only ones in Mower County. They were white and about five feet tall, located in the center of the intersection. The lights would change from red to green, and there were times when cars were lined up bumper-to-bumper waiting for those lights to change.

After dark on Saturday night, the streetlights would go on, and all the stores with their large glass display windows would turn their lights on. Main Street would be all lit up. Some people would shop early, put their things in their cars, and visit with other shoppers. Up and down Main Street men and women and children would gather in small groups to talk with friends and relatives.

Nine o'clock was closing time, except for the barbershops that would stay open until all their customers had gotten their Sunday haircuts. Long after the store lights were turned off, people would still be visiting in their small groups.

Downtown Austin, with one of their central stop signs, back in the day

*Richard Hall, a regular **Minnesota Memories** contributor, lives in Austin with his wife Mickie. Richard has written several local and regional history books that are available at the Mower County Historical Society and the Adams Historical Society.*

Twenty Years Later, Return to the U of M
By Elizabeth "Beth" Becker

After twenty years, I'm back at the University of Minnesota and arrive full of anticipation of my second "first day" of college. This time I drive myself to school.

Dusk is descending on campus in a way I remember, but the University skyline has changed. My GPS locates a new parking ramp near my old dormitory, Comstock Hall. In the 1980s, my roommate had an ancient, white Buick with South Dakota plates and a cherry red interior, which we parked for $1.25 a day under the bridge. Sometimes a metered spot in front of the dorm was taken by a red pickup with "Sire Power" written on the side. It took a South Dakota farm girl to explain the irony of this vehicle repeatedly parking outside the women's dorm.

One Sunday evening during a snowstorm, six of us hiked into Dinkytown because McDonald's was giving away holiday drinking glasses and someone wanted a set. They gave one per person, and we carried them home like Faberge eggs down the snow-covered stone steps alongside Coffman Union, the most important building on campus.

Tonight, climbing the stairs leaves me winded, but I am eager to open the doors to the Union's renowned $30,000,000 renovation. Twenty years ago the main floor was dark and malodorous, with Spanish-restaurant-tiles encircling a hub of vending machines. Now the back of the building opens onto a beautiful terrace overlooking the river bluffs.

The fourth floor crash zone for commuters was a place to sleep on vinyl cubes between classes, headsets on. Millions of dollars later, couches and chairs are still vinyl, but students are tethered to iPods and laptops. You could buy a sub sandwich and a Coke for $2 then, and tonight I am hard pressed to scrape up $1.50 for a drink. The bookstore has been conveniently relocated to the Union, but I miss the old, sprawling, remote location, and the way new freshmen found their way through campus using maps on the backs of their bright goldenrod folders.

I purchase my textbook and head toward the bridge spanning the Mississippi, connecting the east and west banks, but am momentarily confused. There is now a large silver art museum between the bridge and myself. Its facade reminds me of the way some restaurants make a tinfoil swan to carry your take-home food, and I make a few false starts before finding the new pathway to the bridge. A chill nips the air, but the bridge's interior walkway is now heated. I choose to walk outside like the old days, but find myself lagging behind younger students, marveling at the fact that I used to cross this bridge four times a day.

Poignantly missing are a man who used to sell hot cinnamon rolls for a dollar and a homeless man nicknamed Birdman because he always crossed the bridge muttering, with arms outstretched as if he would take flight at any moment. I fight the urge to stretch out my arms in celebration of his memory.

Finally, the west bank is again under my feet! A mass of twisted bike lanes appears on the concrete. "Is this really necessary?" I mutter as I try to nonchalantly contemplate proper crossing procedure. Necessity becomes quickly apparent as two bikers whiz by, heading different directions. Blegen Hall appears unchanged inside, but I keep looking for the big hair, leggings and punk rockers of the '80s. I sink into my desk thanking the powers-that-be that I am not the oldest one in the room.

It is very dark when I cross back over the bridge, but the lamps glow invitingly. I wonder if I should be afraid or call an escort, but feel strangely at home. At the end of the bridge I gaze into the windows of Comstock Hall. The stars make it seem like a snow-globe circa 1983. My old window on the fifth floor is illuminated, and I beg the curtains to open. There are things I want to scream to my 18-year-old self: Insist on pre-natal vitamins! Make Mike have an electrocardiogram! Don't build a stucco house! Cut ties with mother! Learn another language!

Nothing happens, which is probably good because I'd be shocked to see my 18- year-old face looking out at the bridge and into the night. I re-power my cell phone and turn toward the ramp, my ears straining for the bagpipe music that used to emanate at odd hours from under this end of the bridge.

Victoria resident Beth Becker shares her life with her husband, two children, and two dogs. This is her second published piece.

Fry Bread Love
By Pauline Danforth

I love fry bread. I love the bustle of mothers, aunts and grandmothers kneading and stretching dough into elongated donut-shaped fry bread. I love the oily smell of bread frying, the kitchen tinged with grease and flour. I love the taste of fry bread lathered with creamy butter, with bold purple jam and sweet, sticky honey. I love the sensual feel of the dough as I knead and shape it. I love fry bread *way* too much.

This wouldn't be a problem except recently I decided to learn the art of making fry bread, which means I am eating more of it. I'm also learning now because I am the mother and the auntie; I give the hugs and I feed my family. I'm learning because many of my best fry bread makers are gone, either dead or moved away, and I want to carry on this tradition. Every Indian woman, at some level, has this urge to learn the art of making fry bread. From a very young age, we've watched our female relatives make bread, nourishing their families. All our lives we've heard talk about how good so-and-so's fry bread is and how another woman's bread resembles rocks.

My love affair with bread began with my grandmother, affectionately called Mom by all her grandchildren. Mom made her bread in a wood-fueled stove in her four-room tar paper house on the reservation. She made "Indian bread," what Canadian tribes call bannock. Indian bread is like fry bread except instead of two or three inches of oil, it is fried with just a coating in a thick cast-iron skillet. She would knead her bread in a big tin bowl, a dish towel tied around her generous middle. The flour was dusted on the oilskin tablecloth and caked dry on her strong brown hands. My cousins and I would break off a piece and run outside to play, chasing one another around my uncle's 1960s era Studebaker or maybe leaning against the woodpile next to the front door.

Sometimes the smells coming from Mom's kitchen drove us grandkids away. She would hull corn and make hominy by boiling the kernels in lye water. The smell permeated her house and wafted outside. This task took a good part of the day. My cousins and I would pinch our noses and run down the road to climb trees or explore the fields out back. Years later, when I followed the powwow circuit from Wisconsin to North

Dakota, I served hominy soup to tottering grannies who complimented me on how good it tasted as I kicked empty cans out of view.

My mother did not make bread. Instead, she specialized in pies–apple, pumpkin, cherry, and blueberry fresh from Del Monte cans onto her homemade crusts. As a child, I would invite my friends over to bake alongside my mother. She would give us miniature pie tins to fill and bake. Years later, when I was an adult, she made cheesecakes for my infrequent visits to her home in Minneapolis from up north, where I was living the powwow life. Days before my arrival, she would gather the ingredients and assemble the cheesecake to celebrate my visit.

I almost learned to make fry bread from Helen. We worked side-by-side on the powwow trail, going to weekend powwows and selling food to the dancers, drummers and spectators. Helen, who was dry and yeasty like the bread she made, was 100% Norwegian. Her story is she ran away from her staid farmer husband, hung out with Indians, partied heartily with them, and in return became part of the extended family of many of them, including me. I met her when she was in her 60s and I was in my 30s, both us of having put aside our partying ways.

Helen made truly awesome fry bread. She had learned it from her friend Connie, who was the mother of my then-partner Joey in the powwow concession business. Helen, Joey and I sold fry bread, Indian tacos, hominy soup and soda pop at powwows nearly every weekend from June to August, traveling from Wisconsin to North Dakota. We converted a school bus into a kitchen on wheels, complete with propane stoves, soda dispenser, popcorn maker, and refrigerator. Helen mixed and kneaded the fry bread in the morning, and I stood watch and listened as she explained the chemistry of bread making, why yeast needed to be warm, how sugar fed the yeast and why the bread rose. I was lulled by her voice, comforted by her caring, and transported back to the times I watched my grandmother make bread.

Helen made enormous batches of dough. After it rose once, we put it into the refrigerator for a couple of hours until powwow time. Then Helen and I would explore the area, one time climbing up Grand Portage's Hat Mountain to get a birds-eye view of the grounds below, and sometimes just visiting other concessionaires who followed the same powwow circuit. Once when Helen and I returned to the fry bread bus, the dough had crept over the pan and pushed open the refrigerator door.

Aunt Jennie makes good fry bread. When she lived nearby, she would make loaves and loaves of crusty bread and pans of fry bread. I would happily accept her invitation to stop by after work for some warm bread lathered with butter. We talked about her teaching me to make bread, but it never happened, and then she moved back to the reservation. Auntie appreciates relatives who enjoy the food she prepares. She equates a good eater to a person with good health. She often comments with pride that her granddaughter can eat a pile of meatloaf for dinner and be hungry again before bedtime. This child is maybe 3 feet tall and 100 pounds!

Last summer, Cherokee/Muskogee writer Suzan Shown Harjo caused a stir when she dared suggest Indian people give up fry bread because it is ruining their health. She wrote a newspaper column promising to give up fry bread and asking other Indians to do the same for the sake of avoiding diabetes and other killers that claim the lives of our relatives. To put it mildly, this caused quite a stir. True, each piece is loaded with fat and calories (estimated 700 calories and 27 grams of fat), but fry bread is a tradition, her readers said. They got all riled up and wrote back defending their decision to eat fry bread. She went off the deep end in this same column, picked up by the Associated Press, when she likened fry bread to "hard-core porn with no redeeming qualities."

The bigger issue is that Indian people equate hospitality and caring for one's family with hearty eating. You show your love by providing ample meals for your family; you show your appreciation by eating what is put before you. Indian people also equate fry bread with identity. If you are Indian, you either know how to make fry bread or certainly appreciate the taste of a good piece of fry bread. A popular t-shirt on the powwow circuit says "FBI-Fry Bread Indian."

Just as Harjo couldn't change the minds of the Indian people, I can't change my aunt's view that a good eater is a healthy person. Unlike Harjo, who sees the connection between obesity and the slow, hard death from diabetes, my aunt will continue to see hearty eating as a sign of well being.

My aunt has the fry bread (and good cooking) gene, as does my cousin Mary. Now and again Mary comes to my house to fry up a batch. She says she gets nervous when someone watches her, and this makes her bread fail. Last time she was over, I tested her assertion and found excuses to tidy up the kitchen and visit while she worked, gossiping to distract her from commenting on my presence. "Did you hear about cousin Mousie and how his old lady kicked him out? And about cousin Spaghetti…Auntie says he is back in jail for selling weed." (Yeah, they have crazy nicknames, but that's another story.) So our conversation flowed and despite my presence, Mary's fry bread came out perfect– yellow-brown, big and wide and oh-so-sweet lathered with honey.

Both Mary and Kim prove that fry bread making is truly an art. Many Indians proudly wear the title"fry bread queen." Some powwows, including the Navaho Fair, have fry bread making contests. Indian people write poems about fry bread, or like me, write stories about fry bread. Type "fry bread" in your computer search engine, and you are sure to get thousands of links ranging from Home and Garden TV to reservation community groups selling cookbooks.

From my travels, I've discovered that Navahos tend to make their fry bread, also called sopapillas, large and flat, like honey-colored Frisbees. Woodland tribes like the Ojibwe prefer them the size of a saucer, thick and puffy. Heart-healthy Indians will use canola oil rather than Crisco or substitute whole-wheat flour, but that just doesn't taste like fry bread.

A true fry bread connoisseur like me will go to a powwow simply to taste the fry bread. Even before I visit the circle of vendors camped around the powwow arena selling silver and beaded jewelry and t-shirts, I check out the fry bread stands. If I see a cousin or a friend, I will ask them to help me narrow down the field to maybe their top three contenders. We talk about whether this one is too doughy, this other one was served cold, that one was dry and tough, or this other one too salty. I always sample two or three before I make my decision.

Indian people believe that fry bread, really any food, tastes extra good when it is made with a good heart, with love. Certainly nothing beats the bread made by the skillful hands of my grandmother, friend

Helen, aunt Jennie, and cousin Mary. They knead lots and lots of love into the dough, letting it rise to great proportions and spreading it around to me and everyone else they love.

Lately I decided to spread my own love. I made a pledge to make fry bread every weekend. Some fry breads call for baking powder, others for yeast. The bread has to rise properly, and it should taste just a little bit salty and a little bit sweet, even before the toppings that could be taco stuff or sweets like honey, blueberries, or sugar and cinnamon.

In the past my friends and relatives have called my bread "door stops" or "statues," or other such names. This criticism even comes from friends who don't make fry bread. They laugh indulgently at my feeble attempts. I'm serious now. I do this scientifically, not in Helen's fashion but in my own. I spread four or five fry bread recipes before me and have my handy meat thermometer ready to test the hot milk that feeds the yeast. I knead and knead the dough until it is pliable but not too sticky, then leave it alone in a warm place for an hour or two. Then comes the tricky part of heating the Crisco (no other oil will do) to the right temperature so that the bread gets a light crust but doesn't penetrate too deeply.

Yes, fry bread done right is a well-deserved guilty pleasure, but the real joy is sharing the cooking and the bread with those you love. Gather your sisters, cousins and aunts. Add flour, yeast and Crisco, and you have the makings of a really good time!

Indian bread expert Nancy Kettle, Pauline's Grandma, at the White Earth Reservation.

Pauline Danforth is an Ojibwe from the White Earth Reservation. She has worked in higher education for twenty years as an advisor, instructor and administrator. Her stories about her Ojibwe ancestors and family have been published in local and national anthologies.

Marsh Secret
By Wendy A. Skinner

Most people who live around here are familiar with the common activities of the marsh, but a year ago our family discovered a secret the marsh holds deep in its heart, a secret only briefly revealed and entrusted to us. We live only two blocks from Minneapolis, yet our property backs up to a large marsh, referred to by city officials as a giant storm sewer. It collects runoff from the masses of asphalt and highway to the west and eventually deposits water into Lake Calhoun to the east. But to its animal residents, the marsh is a sanctuary, a hiding spot from the city, a rest stop on the migration route. As a rite of spring, shy painted turtles and large tank-like snappers voyage up neighborhood streets to dig nests and lay eggs into the slopes of our front lawns.

Winter was mild one year, enough to cause my 9-year-old to bite his nails three weeks before Christmas while anticipating the arrival of the city water truck. At last, within a day or two, the temperature took a nosedive and the water truck began appearing. Every day it drove in circles at the park as it sprayed layer upon layer of water onto the ground. And, as the neighborhood rink froze, so did the ice on the marsh.

Wendy's marsh

I had my eye on the marsh. It hadn't snowed much before the initial freeze—a good sign. That week, snow blanketed the frozen surface by only a few inches. Within two weeks with cold weather, we'd have ideal ice on the marsh for skating.

But the marsh is a tricky and dangerous place to be on in the winter. The outlet never completely freezes. Because of the industrial runoff, there is always an underlying warm current snaking its way through the marsh to the outlet. One morning the ice and snow could appear flawlessly white, cold, and frozen, but by late afternoon a dark streak would have grown down the center channel, stretching its fingers into the outlet, spilling steaming ripples of black water over the dam.

In spring our family canoed through the marsh's winding channel, surprising nesting Canada geese and schools of large orange goldfish gone wild. I'd gone cross-country skiing by myself on the marsh in the past, enjoying the forgiving flatness and smoothness of the snow covered ice. But I had yet to ice skate the marsh. This year, I thought, this year we'll try it.

While the kids attended their last few days of school before winter break, I had a morning free to give in to temptation. I pulled on my white Sorrel boots and my sturdiest gloves and headed for the outlet with my favorite yellow snow shovel. The outlet was still open, but the ice several feet from it was solid. Its snowy surface was unblemished. I ventured from the wooded bank through stiff brown cattails and set my shovel down where the frozen water met the edge of the reeds. Shhhhh, the shovel peeled off a layer of thin snow, curling it over on itself like quilt batting. As I shoveled, I zigzagged toward the center of the marsh, around the corner, and out of sight from the outlet.

Soon I came to a junction. The main fifteen-foot-wide channel, with its warm dark waters churning beneath, went to the right. A narrower twisting channel veered to the left. I glanced at my watch. My time was up. I had to turn back for the day.

I couldn't return soon afterward. However, on the following nights, winter's luck was with us. With single digit lows, the marsh ice thickened every night until Christmas Eve. That night, after dinner, I packed hot cocoa and chocolate chip cookies and put them with two folding lawn chairs onto our old metal runner sled. In the moonless night we made our way to the marsh's edge, walking through the woods in our skates like clumsy newborn deer.

Now four shovels scraped the ice. My husband led the line, and I was second with the sled in tow. Soon, our children raced ahead of me giggling and chasing each other down the freshly shoveled path, reminding me of Hans Brinker stories of skating races down the frozen canals of Holland.

We passed the junction and blazed a new path through the undisturbed snow of the narrow left channel. We approached an immense expanse of flat, uninterrupted snow. The channel dead-ended here, in the center of the marsh. With droplets of condensation on our scarves, we paused, hearing only our heavy breathing, and examined our surroundings, a broad area surrounded by walls of tall cattails, carpeted with five inches of flawless snow, and a ceiling of blackness sprinkled with stars.

We spent the next hour in the still night air skating and plowing a center rink, an outer racetrack and numerous twisting, connecting pathways. My husband and I traded off snowplow duty, which was never finished since snow inevitably was scattered in all directions following a collision or loss of balance. My son and his younger 6-year-old sister stopped often to sip the hot cocoa, take a bite of cookie and rest their feet while they sat in the lawn chairs. Snow angels magically appeared on the edges of the racetrack as if to guard against additional collisions.

When I had retired from snowplow duty for the last time, I rested my own feet while I sat in the lawn chair. Taking my hat off to cool my sweaty forehead, I looked up and saw a glinting flash of light in the sky. Focussing more carefully, I realized that the whole sky directly above us was dimly but noticeably set afire with the Northern Lights as if they were flaring from Polaris, the northern star itself. Within moments all of us stood still, frozen, necks craned upward. Snow muffled exclamations were soon followed by pointing mittens and gloves, excited chatter, and then the realization that our toes were too cold to feel.

Tucking the children in their beds that night, we whispered about skating again on Christmas night and how we would widen the race track, add more pathways to our well established maze, and pack sandwiches for a night time picnic.

In the morning, while the scent of pancakes and sausages still lingered in the air and the last of the gifts were unwrapped, we could see water steadily dripping from the roof of the house just outside the window. A warm front had slipped in during the late night.

Not bothering to put on my jacket, I took a short walk down to the outlet of the marsh to survey the previous night's snow plowing. Snow sank into forbidding shadowy streaks from the outlet's open water, and last night's glassy skating trail was now soft and bumpy. Our skating path was looking less like a trail and more like just another aberration in the marsh's melting snowy surface. The marsh's secret was now our secret too. And it was as though overnight the marsh had put its finger to its lips and whispered, "Shhh."

Minneapolis writer Wendy Skinner is anticipating the 2007 debut of her first book, **Infinity and Zebra Stripes: Raising Highly Gifted Children***, published by Great Potential Press. She enjoys growing flowers to sell at the Excelsior Farmers' Market and teaching writing to elementary school children. She and her husband have two children and various pets.*

I Hope She's Not Still Waiting
By Harvey Ronglien

I grew up in the Minnesota State School for Dependent and Neglected Children in Owatonna. We got three square meals a day and lots of exercise, but we didn't learn many practical skills that kids who grow up in a regular family usually learn from their folks in their teens–like how to manage money or how to drive a car. I enlisted in the Army right after I turned 18 in 1945 and spent a little time working for Uncle Sam in Italy right after World War II, but when I got out I was still wet behind the ears. I returned to Owatonna, where I planned to get a job and conquer the world.

Bob Reynolds, another State Schooler, was a friend of mine, and we had one adventure I will always remember. Still somewhat flush with discharge money and free from the restrictions of military control, Bob and I felt invincible. One day Bob, a carefree soul with an incomprehensible thought process, came to me with a problem. He had met the girl of his dreams, a Waseca girl, who in his eyes was as beautiful as Betty Grable, the pin-up favorite of many GIs. He had asked her out for a date, and he needed my help.

He had a couple of minor roadblocks to overcome before said date. But since we were young and invincible, we did not consider these hurdles to be insurmountable. Bob saw himself as a suave, worldly man who was scheduled to knock on the young lady's door the next evening and escort her into a world she had never seen, in a style she was unaccustomed to. Up to this point, his plan seemed realistic for a guy of his age and status.

But barriers suddenly came into focus. In rapid order, these problems included the fact that Bob didn't have a car, he didn't have a driver's license, and he had never driven a car. Waseca is about fifteen miles from Owatonna. He asked me if I would chauffeur him, but I didn't have a car. I did not have a license either, and I had never driven a car. Bob and I had grown up in the same place, a home where there was no father figure to take boys out and teach them to drive when we turned 15. We were a few years behind other young men our age, at least as far as driving was concerned.

The plan we concocted was ingenious. We would ignore the law. Who needed a license? We had just won the war; we could certainly buy a car. His pockets bulged with green. Everybody else was driving a car so it couldn't be that difficult. Side by side we confidently marched into Mulken's Used Car Lot. After surveying the inventory and taking no test drive (we weren't much for details), we completed the transaction and proudly climbed into our vehicle of choice. Bob drove, and his plan was to deposit me at my place and then continue on with his evening's plans.

Of course, the car had standard transmission, and neither of us had any idea how to drive it. After grinding the gears severely, he wisely left it in one gear and maneuvered his way out of Mulken's to my little corner of the world. As he arrived at my residence, he mistakenly hit the gas pedal instead of the brake. Confusion reigned supreme as we lurched forward, jumped the curb and slammed into a sturdy oak.

Slightly flustered but uninjured and undaunted, we jumped from the car to measure the damages. Well, they were fairly extreme so adjustments had to be made. After further pondering our situation, we decided the car had to go. We limped back to Mulken's, and at a substantial loss to Bob's finances, they agreed to take the battered vehicle back. My friend had owned his first car for all of thirty minutes. As we left the car lot on foot, we looked back and saw Mulken's crew watching us with confused looks.

Bob thought he should notify the young lady about his transportation predicament, but my pal didn't know Juliet's last name. How could we contact her? We could see no honorable way out. Consequently the seeds of a healthy relationship had been nipped in the bud before they could blossom into lasting love. Or maybe fate took over and rescued the fair maiden from a life of distress. We'll never know.

This is an excerpt from Harvey Ronglien's book, **A Boy From C-11: Case 9164.** *Harvey and his wife are curators and tour guides at the State School Orphanage Museum in Owatonna.*

Young Harvey

Snowshoeing the Kadunce
By Lin Calof

It's winter in Northern Minnesota. Snow is banked three feet high along the sides of Highway 61, and a foot of fresh fallen snow blankets the driveway. It is a sticky snow that clings to the branches of trees, road signs and even the stalks of weeds in the ditches. The trees lining the driveway form a white canopy so that it feels as though I'm driving into one of those sugared-egg dioramas that we used to admire each Easter when I was a child.

I park the car in front of the house and walk down to Lake Superior. A thin sheath of ice has formed on the lake's surface, pinning it to the shore. Usually the waves clash violently with rocks and ice must form farther out, away from its angry edges. Today it is still, and it seems as though I can see the ice form, knitting itself together crystal by crystal across the lake.

Walking the shoreline, I carefully pick my way, step by step, selecting dry patches on the rock so I won't slip into the frigid water. I squat to inspect a bubble of air, kidney shaped, trapped under the ice on a rock. Rivulets of water pulsate along its edges, under the ice, slithering down toward the lake. It reminds me of something I saw in biology class in high school as I peered into the lens of a microscope: a protozoa swimming across a glass slide. Life, where it seemed there was none.

I think of November gales that give the lake her voice, her language of crash and gurgle and sputter, and I stop to listen to what the lake might say today . . . she whispers . . . *ping* . . . *tinkle* . . . a sound like breaking glass. Off the shore at the edge of the ice, I watch as water rocks in response to something that has happened farther out in the lake, and as it rolls into the ice, small splinters and shards stick up at odd angles, the sun glinting off the sharp blades formed by undulating water. Sunset arrives earlier on the North Shore than in the Cities, and as daylight fades, I'm chilled. But before I head into the house, I watch the sun disappear over the hill, like a copper penny dropping into a slot.

I wake to sunshine streaming in the window the next morning; blue sky is framed by white birch. Nuthatches and chickadees hop from branch to branch, and a red-headed woodpecker is working on the dead birch near the woodpile. The snow is blindingly white and its surface temporarily unbroken.

I pad downstairs in my slippers to let the dog out and start the coffee. Kirby chases a red squirrel up a tree where it chatters and shakes its tale at him in a reproof. I start my day here at Selah as I have many other mornings, lying on my back, looking up at the pine ceiling to identify figures in the grains of wood, like when I was a kid and I picked out shapes in the clouds. There are two alligators kissing, a mouse, a heart, a fox, a wolf, a man-o-war and even an owl. There is a wood duck sitting at the edge of a pond. I am certain that I see a mother duck, trailed by its duckling. Or is it a loon? There's a mother eagle and her baby straight up from the door frame. The square dark part is her chest and an angle jutting from the square is her neck. Her eye is a dark spot in the wood. Well, maybe it's an abstract eagle.

Today I decided to snowshoe the Kadunce River, angling through the narrow canyon toward the waterfall. After a breakfast of banana-oatmeal pancakes, I jumped in the truck and headed east. Kirby was anxious to explore and smiled at me from the back seat. I was hoping he would behave and stay away from the open bowls of water that we'd encounter along the river. I parked. Kirby bounded from the car, and I strapped on my snowshoes. I followed the trail to the frozen river—the dog running ahead, and then running back to check on me. This is how we hike. He gets twice as much exercise as I do—which is good, because he's a Brittney, which is like a springer spaniel on drugs. Unfortunately, when he runs he gets thirsty, and the small holes of open water look inviting. Very tempting. Very dangerous. I have to keep calling his name to keep him on track. He has a short memory.

I dig in with my snowshoes and hike up a small cascade, feeling like a spy with access to the world's top secrets. In the spring, I follow the Superior Hiking Trail at the edge of the river that veers off into forest of old cedar, white pine, spruce and birch. In summer, I pick wild blueberries and make them into tarts back at Selah. But in winter, when the river is frozen, I can explore its secret places, the places where over thousands of years it has cut through the rock and scooped out the now frozen basin at the bottom of the waterfall. It seems a more intimate exploration.

Walking the river's frozen surface, I imagine the water flowing beneath my feet, over the rocks, cascading, turning, curling, unfurling toward the lake. In the summer, the open places are deep pools, places where the water swirls and swells or spins in a tight vortex, creating little meringue cakes of foam that bob on the surface.

Farther up the river, the passage through the canyon constricts. I can stretch out my arms on both sides and touch the stone walls. The rhyolite walls rise 75 feet overhead and look like layered tablets of stone. Around the next curve, there is a small heap of rock that has tumbled down the gorge. The rock is oxidized and crumbles easily; I avoid using the walls for support.

I hear water rushing in the distance and know that I'm approaching one of the waterfalls; it's breathtaking. Near the top, frozen billows of water hang in a solid white mass of ice, gradually thinning as I follow the path of the water with my eyes, until it is a glassy sheath through which I can see the water rushing. The last foot is open, and the water gushes and splutters into a hole in the basin.

I squat and watch the water pounding into the hole, feeling the spray on my cheeks and hair and the force of the water reverberating in my chest. Standing here in the frozen basin, it seems as though I have found an arctic bath, a place where ancient man stood, as beads of water gathered on his skin, running in rivulets down his legs before he plunged into the frigid pool. The air in the basin is still, the canyon walls form a great wind barrier, but still, I shiver in the damp.

As I call Kirby back from the rushing water, my voice echoes off canyon walls, and for a moment he is confused, looking up, this way and that, trying to find the source, as though small gnomes live here and taunt him. In the echoes, I hear the ancient days calling, the hundreds of thousands of years that the water has dripped, then streamed, then cascaded over the topography, cutting its way deep into this ravine, hiding the river here, tucked away in the woods and the rock.

Lin Calof, who lives in Burnsville. is working on a memoir called **Crazy for You.**

Wintertime During the Great Depression
By Lloyd Deuel

During the Depression in the early 1930s, many newlywed people had a difficult time because there were no jobs. They were invited to live with relatives. Most people thought this practice was the natural thing to do, as everyone was willing to help out during those hard economic times. I really enjoyed having more grownups being around, and I bonded with them.

My mother's sister Emma and her husband Louie lived with us first. I barely remember when my cousin Gwen was born in our house. It was February, 1932 and very cold, but not much snow. The roads were open, and some of my mother's sisters were there to see the baby. It was decided that the house had to be kept warm at night, and my dad and Louie stayed up to keep the furnace stoked up. I learned later that they played cribbage, and the loser would have to go down and throw more wood on the fire. We had a gravity type furnace in the basement and a wood-burning cook stove in the kitchen. The house did not have any insulation, and the doors of rooms that were not needed were kept closed.

"The roads were open," meant that cars and trucks could still get to town. There were no snowplows at that time, and after big snowfalls the only way to travel on the roads was by horse-pulled bobsleds. Farm people did not have money for luxuries, and town visits were for life's necessities.

The next couple who lived with us was my mother's sister, Eunice and her husband Mearl. I thought it was great to have more people in the house. Winter was not a good time to be moving, but in the spring they could find a place of their own.

My dad's brother Percy and his wife Florence were the last newly married couple who lived with us for a time. My dad had a Model T truck, and he hauled wood and he had a cream route. He picked up cream from neighbors and hauled it to the Foreston Creamery. Extra help on the farm was always appreciated when my dad was tending to his other endeavors.

Wild game was plentiful, and my dad was a marksman and hunter. I think that most meat we ate was because of my dad's hunting skills. No meat went to waste at our house as any extra meat was either shared with neighbors or my mother canned it for future use. I loved canned venison in the summer when fresh meat was hard to keep for any length of time.

Winters were severe both in snowfall and low temperatures. In midwinter of 1934-35 the house that I was born in burned to the ground in Foreston. My grandparents had moved to the house across the street, and fire sparks threatened their house. My dad was called, and he started for Foreston, but his car got stuck and stalled in snow. He had to come back home, and he learned that the temperature was minus forty degrees by the Foreston thermometers. The Foreston volunteer fire department had no success trying to put the fire out. One of the firemen, Hugh Amo, told me that he was on the roof of a neighboring house with a fire hose. When he signaled for pressure on his hose, the response was a small squirt because the hose was frozen. If the water had not frozen, he thought they could have saved the house. As it was they barely got their truck back in the warm fire barn in time to save the tank and valves from freezing.

With all the wood burning stoves that heated these old houses, green wood would sometimes get mixed in with the dry wood. Green wood would create a creosote coating in the chimneys, and when it hardened and a fresh fire was started in the stove, it would cause a chimney fire. If a chimney fire was not detected early, it would cause a backup and spread upwards and start the roof on fire. I was told this is the reason that some of the old houses burned down, and the barn and outbuildings often outlasted the houses.

There were many house fires in the early and midwinter. A tragic stove fire in a house happened when my dad was young and still living with his parents. It happened during a snowstorm. A neighbor couple was in the barn doing milking in the morning. When they finished, and came out of the barn they found their house was gone and it was still smoldering. Their three kids and their grandpa vanished in the flames. When we lived on the Deuel farm, it was a rule that if both my parents had to be in the barn doing milking, they would bundle me up and take me to the barn with them.

Woodcutting was the main occupation for farmers in the early winter after deer hunting was over. My dad used his Model T truck to haul wood for us and for neighbors. Hauling wood meant piling long, thin logs or poles too small for lumber onto the back of his truck and trailer and dumping it where the woodpile would be. His cousins, the Axt brothers, had a huge circular saw mounted on a platform powered by a steam engine, later replaced by an engine salvaged from a Model T car. They would go from one farmyard to another and saw these poles into about 15-inch lengths for the stoves, creating in each yard a mountain of sawed wood.

At first I could only watch this interesting activity from a window in the house because Mother would not allow me to be near this dangerous work. There came a time when I could get closer, but not be in the way of all these men who gathered to share this work. It was extremely cold, and this was when I noticed that with all of their runny noses, the men did not use handkerchiefs like I was instructed to use. They wore leather mittens with wool liners called "choppers." They would place a chopper thumb on one side of the nose and blow and then on the other side. They always seemed to hit the snow where they aimed. I thought this was very neat and clever. I practiced and imitated these men the best that I could, but made a mess of myself. I thought if I practiced enough I would become adept. When my mother saw my jacket, she immediately put a stop to this. Mother was adept at watching for these new adventures.

In 1935 I started kindergarten at District 6, Pleasant View School in Milo Township, Mille Lacs County. Kindergarten started the last six weeks of the school year. In the fall of 1935, I started first grade. My parents bought me school supplies for kindergarten. A box of crayons cost 10 cents, and consisted of seven crayons. That fall my mother discovered that all of the crayons were broken and worn out, and she had to buy me a new box. The following year the second graders did not need crayons, but that year the boxes were enhanced to twelve crayons. My classmates and I were very disappointed.

My mother bought me a new winter jacket, boots, shoes, pants and shirts to start first grade. After school started she felt that I should have a light jacket to wear until it got colder. She sent to Sears Roebuck, a mail order company, for a nifty light jacket. This jacket was quite pricey, but she thought it was justified because she only had one child to buy for. She was extremely disappointed when the jacket came in the mail. It had a zipper instead of buttons. She complained that a little boy would break the zipper, but if it had buttons she could always sew new buttons on. The jacket cost nearly a dollar. She didn't know if it would be worth all that postage to send it back. We kept the jacket and I soon outgrew it. It was passed on to younger cousins, again and again. The zipper outlasted the jacket.

When winter set in, the roads became passable only with horses and bobsled. It was extremely hard to walk in bobsled ruts or horse tracks. The alternative was to ski to school, which every kid and the teachers did as well. My skis were the ones that my dad had used, and they were homemade and nearly ten feet long. He made bindings out of cut up tire inner tubes. It took a lot of patience to navigate these monsters, but it was better than trying to walk in horse step prints.

There was a rule in School District 6 that kids less than 8 years old and before they started third grade should not be required to help milk cows. My mother did a lot of debating this rule on the telephone party line. Some thought that little kids should not be "coddled," while Esther Deuel said that little kids should have a chance to be kids. At school we first and second graders had to listen to third and fourth grade boys boast as to how many cows they milked morning and night (by hand). Finally a savvy fourth grade girl told us if we paid attention to our arithmetic we would figure out that these boys claimed to milk more cows than what was on their farm.

Recently I attended an all-school reunion at District 6. The school district was formed in 1869 and closed in 1970. This was the school that Grandpa Deuel attended with his siblings when they moved to the Deuel Farm in 1885 and later my dad and his siblings attended. The reason these one and two room country schools were so successful was the small class size. When a teacher has only ten or fifteen kids to teach, she can give them undivided attention. It has been proven that the most important years of a person's education are the first three grades.

During the Depression years, parents were forced to move a great deal because of economic hard times. It was said that the children were the ones who paid the price for changing schools often. One of the tools that the teacher used was "mentoring." She would assign older kids to help the younger ones in their studies. The girls especially loved this chance to "play school." They would tell us to pay attention or they would tell our mothers. We knew that they were well acquainted with our moms. Later, when it was my turn to be a mentor, I would tell the boy to pay attention or we wouldn't let him play ball with us. He would have to be able count balls and strikes. Both approaches seemed to be very effective.

I think it was the winter of 1936-37 that we had a tremendous amount of snow. The roads were impassable early and stayed that way until spring. There was a neighbor who was sick, and at first the neighbor women were consulted. The doctor was called to visit the person, but he could not reach the farm because of the snow. He recommended the person be taken to the hospital.

The doctor called the Mille Lacs County highway department, and they agreed to send a snowplow. The next problem was how to transport the person behind the snowplow. It was suggested that Ira Deuel could make the trip because he had new 1936 Terraplane pickup that was really good in snow.

The first snowplows I ever saw were the two that pulled into our yard to plow out the garage so that my dad's pickup could get out. The county had just bought two of these new plows, and they sent both in case one got stalled. They had front wheel drive, and it was a novelty for everyone to see both front and back wheels spinning at the same time. My dad made the trip to the Princeton hospital with no problem, and our neighbor was treated. After the county bought these snowplows, the county roads were plowed. The township roads, which the District 6 School and nearly all of the pupils lived on, were not plowed so we still had to ski to school.

Lloyd Deuel, who grew up near Foreston and Milaca, has contributed to ***Minnesota Memories*** *books since 2002. He is a retired machinist living in Brooklyn Center.*

Crossing Deer Creek
By Alyce "Penny" Jacobsen

Deer Creek meanders through a wooded valley in southeast Minnesota's Fillmore County. Jake and I and our family have enjoyed its scenery, limestone bluffs, and wildflowers for more than forty years. Part of its charm is its inaccessibility—its feeling of wilderness. Our property is on the far side of the river, and getting across was often a challenge.

When the river level was low, we could drive through. Our boys made jokes about washing the car's belly and watching out for alligators. During high water season, we sometimes waded through in our hip boots with picnic supplies in a backpack. Sometimes we would leave the car on the road and hike over high ground, thus avoiding the river completely. In the winter when the river was mostly, but not completely ice covered, we would use skis or snowshoes to get to the other side.

Penny Jacobsen crossing Deer Creek

A few years ago things changed. Tom Kuehn bought part of the valley and remodeled his cabin so that he could use it all year. He improved the road, and he and his helpers built two bridges using logs and miscellaneous lumber. Since our land is beyond his, we enjoyed using those bridges too. However, floodwaters in the spring of 2006 washed out both bridges. One is still missing, but Tom rebuilt the other bridge with a steep, rocky incline leading to a deck of logs and planks. It is serviceable for pickups, doubtful for cars.

Several times we had friends drive their own cars to the valley, then transfer to the back of our pickup to cross the river. We preferred having them ride without risking damaging their cars on the bridge. But this plan doesn't work for all our guests. Our young granddaughter was planning to visit us one time last year, and we thought it would be fun to hunt fossils and have a picnic near Deer Creek with her. Since three people do not fit in the cab of our truck, and transporting someone fifty miles in the back of the pickup is out of the question, I really wanted to know if we could take our car, a Toyota Camry, over that bridge.

Tuesday afternoon Jake and I were in the Chatfield area visiting a friend, and on our way home we decided to stop at the valley. "Good," I thought, "We'll check out the water level and the bridge and see if there's anything blooming."

After unlocking the gate, Jake drove slowly down the hill and stopped in front of the bridge. We both decided that it looked as if we could drive across. It was definitely not a fast, careless decision, but it turned out to be a big mistake—an error in judgment. At the top of the slope we heard a loud "whump," and the engine stopped. Jake let the car roll backward to level ground and tried unsucsessfully several times to start it. Jake looked under the car, then under the hood and said, "This part has been knocked loose. We're not going anywhere." Really–that's all he said. He did not say, "#**$0#&#!" And I did not sit down and cry.

I said, "I'll put on my walking shoes and go find a neighbor with a phone." Jake stayed with the car, and I headed up the hill, out our gate, then down the gravel road toward a farm place about half a mile away. As I hurried along the dusty road, I became thirsty. Although I had eaten an early supper with lemonade and taken a recent drink from our travel water bottle, my thoughts were not of car trouble, but of how thirsty I was. I worried about desert wanderers who suffered extreme thirst.

County road #38 has very little traffic, and I was almost to the top of the second hill when I heard a vehicle coming up behind me. I turned, held out my hand, looked desperate, and the driver stopped. He agreed to take me to his house, about two miles away, so I could use the phone. His wife gave me a glass of water and a hug.

We do not carry a cell phone. If we had had one, we could have called Amoco Motor Club and waited for a tow truck to come from Rochester—about thirty miles. That might have worked, but as I was soon to learn, cell phones usually don't work down in valleys. I tried calling Tom Kuehn, our valley neighbor who is a car dealer in Spring Valley. I knew he would lend us a car to drive home and tell us what to do or who to contact to get our Camry repaired.

Answering machines are wonderful in some situations, but frustrating when you really need to reach someone. Glen and Jean McNamara helped me make nine phone calls, and leave seven messages, but none of them connected directly with Tom. Finally (it was now after 7 p.m.), one of Kuehn Motor Company's after-hours employees agreed to wait for us and let us use a car. I had assured him that Tom would approve.

Glen McNamara had finished milking his cows so he delayed his supper and took me back to our valley to get Jake, then drove both of us (his pickup has a little back seat) to Spring Valley. Tom had learned of our predicament and was at his shop waiting with keys to a Buick Park Avenue for us to use. He offered to take care of everything—towing, ordering necessary parts, and having his mechanic fix our car.

Now, three days later, we are on our way home from Spring Valley in our Camry. Trying to cross Deer Creek proved to be a very costly experiment. It cost $1581.65 to learn that we must not drive a car over that bridge.

Alyce "Penny" Jacobsen lives in Albert Lea. A retired speech clinician and grandmother of two, she enjoys reading, writing, traveling and admiring the beauty of wildflowers at her Spring Valley retreat.

Ice Golfing
By Ken Nelson

Most Minnesotans go to Florida, Texas or Arizona to play golf during the winter, but my family and I devised a different way to hit the links when the weather got cold. For several lake freeze-ups in the early 1990s, we were blessed with beautiful, clear, smooth and very safe ice before the snows came. On at least three occasions, we built nine-hole golf courses that covered much of the north section of Albert Lea Lake. Each course had two par-three holes, two par-fives, and five par-fours, with yardage lengths comparable to those on a regular golf course.

We personalized each hole by chopping its shape into the ice, and we inserted a fireplace log in the approximate center of each hole to serve as a flag. The first hole was shaped like the Roman numeral I, about five inches by ten, carved a couple inches down into the ice. The second hole was two ones side by side. Hole three was a triangle, then a square, a pentagon and hexagon for four, five and six. Hole seven looked like the number, and eight was two round holes. Nine looked like the number with a circle and a leg. We used the ice chips from chopping out these shapes to make what you might call a sand trap or hazard. Our cub cadet and trailer served as a golf cart, and we carried a rubber mat with a plastic tee from area to area so that we wouldn't slip while making our shots.

From their home in Woodbury, our lifelong friends, Bobby and Kay, brought bankers, college professors and clergy to our ice golf courses, and together we had some fun times and hilarious happenings. One such happening occurred on the fifth tee-off from the elevated tee box in the woods across the lake. Bob's preacher friend, sizing up the 500-yard hole, selected his driver to propel a solid core ball out over the lake. Upon contact, that ball split in two, and each half played a different tune extremely audibly as they tumbled through the cold afternoon air. I heard the preacher swear as he turned back to us, "Damn, did you guys see and hear that?"

Through many tee-offs, we found that a well-hit low trajectory ball could roll the length of a 400-yard hole on clear ice, but could not make it half way if there was even a small amount of snow. Scores were better than expected because the holes were large, making long putts possible.

After our ice golfing season ended one year, I did not get around to removing the fireplace log flags, and in the spring, I was outside one beautiful morning doing some chores. While in the process of splitting more logs, I observed an eagle soaring high above me. I paused and watched its many circles until my neck rebelled, and I reluctantly returned to the task of splitting wood.

Moments later, I was distracted by a screech, and looking back up I saw the eagle diving at a steep angle toward the center of the lake. His target turned out to be one of the hole-marking logs, and as he neared it at high speed with his talons down, he suddenly pulled up and did a fly by. Whether he thought it was a meal from high in the air I will never know, but he did a swooping turn around and came back to land on the log. The weight of that eagle landing on top of the log sitting on our thawing lake tipped the log, and the bird momentarily sprawled forward onto the ice. I did not resist the temptation to rush back to the house and call Bobby to say, "I got an eagle on the fifth hole today."

Ken Nelson (second from left) and his wife Vera with their Woodbury friends, ice golfing at the sixth hole on Albert Lea Lake.

There Must Be a Better Way to Shoot a Deer
By Ken Nelson

With Minnesota's deer hunting season approaching in the late 1970s, Uncle Ed was adamant about going to the Gunflint Trail one more time to mark his fiftieth year of deer hunting. My dad, Ed's brother, had been the trail boss for most of those years until he passed away in 1952, at which time I became the trail boss and trip arranger.

While I was reluctant to go another year to our old haunts because wolves had decimated the Arrowhead herd to near zero, I was equally reluctant to let Uncle Ed down. I owed him something for my first hunts in the 1940s, when he took me under his wing to train me in the ways of the wily bucks.

While traveling to the trail on this occasion in our last big Cadillac, I so well remembered a story that Uncle Ed often told of one of his first trips to the Gunflint. On his first morning in the bush, a call from Mother Nature had prompted him to set his firearm against a tree and back into a space between a couple of trees. While he was occupied with the task at hand, a deer smelled his rifle and bounded off. The lesson he learned was: Never ever leave your rifle out of reach in the woods.

When we arrived on the trail, we were greeted by a very heavy amount of snow that had fallen several days before. Tops from several spruce had broken off in the storm and plunged top first into the snow. We checked for deer trails as we drove thirty miles to Nor'wester Lodge. In years gone by, there would have been many per mile, but this time there were none.

My daily tasks started with making breakfast. Uncle Ed said I was a great cook. After breakfast I'd scout the outer fringes of our favorite haunts and then cook dinner while planning the afternoon hunt. The evening meal was a lodge-prepared feast.

On the first morning of that year's hunt, while scouting the perimeter trail, I found nothing but timber wolf trails and bedding sites, so my lunch hour appraisal was dismal and without suggestion other than to announce that everyone would be on his own this afternoon.

After washing all the dishes, my brother-in-law, Bobby Jensen, and I decided to just walk up the Gunflint a quarter mile or so, enter the woods a couple hundred yards, and take up separate selected stands and maybe take a much needed nap. My selected stand was about two hundred yards from the trail, within earshot of the occasional vehicles going by. I had walked between two spruce tops that had been spiked into the ground and were still heavily laden with snow. That served as a shield from both the Gunflint and the wind. About thirty feet beyond the spruce treetops was a steep and rugged 15-foot drop off to a fairly open, smallish tree plain.

I took a position of best visibility, just at the upper edge of the drop off and out of the wind, and in a few short minutes got a call from Mother Nature. Remembering Uncle Ed's hard-learned lesson, but thinking it irrelevant with no deer around, I placed my Winchester Magnum against a tree, within easy reach and ready to fire as I lowered my trousers and long johns to ankle level.

With my task nearing completion, I heard the adrenalin rush sound of hoof beats coming from behind the spruce trees, through which I had recently walked. Turning my gaze from the open area ahead of me to the direction of the hoof beats over my right shoulder, I spotted a ten-point buck as he slid to a screeching halt less than thirty feet from me.

Unable to shoulder that Magnum because I could not turn my tethered feet, I touched off one shot as though I was firing a handgun. The Magnum recoil was absorbed not by my shoulder but by my right breast, which stayed black and blue and red and green for several weeks. The powerful impact knocked me completely off balance and all the way to the bottom of the drop off with my ankles still locked in snow packed trousers and long johns. As I checked for bruises and broken bones, I looked back up at my neatly arranged cleaning tissue hanging from a couple of twigs and decided snow and pine needles were my only option.

Redressing in my wet and cold clothing was an unavoidable pursuit, and climbing back up the rocky drop off was an adventure in itself. As if that weren't enough, let's just say that the rifle needed to be cleaned.

This misadventure turned to the usual adrenalin rush when I saw the trophy buck lying dead just behind the two spruce trees he came sliding through. His momentum sliding between the two downed treetops was such that he turned to jump backwards and exposed his head to my arriving bullet, which entered his left cheekbone and exploded his right horn socket.

When Bobby arrived in response to the shot he heard, he found it hard to believe what I told him, but all the evidence was there, very fresh and conclusive. This adventure has been retold and partially demonstrated many times over the years. It's just unfortunate we had no video cams in those days.

Albert Lea native Ken Nelson worked in engineering, product design, research and sales for Scottsman Industries. He and his wife Vera have three daughters and six grandchildren. While laid up with a bad leg a couple of years ago, he started writing his stories, and their numbers continue to grow as time goes by.

A Short Tie Affair
By Ken Nelson

One of my fond memories from our Gunflint home away from home took place when the Nor'wester Lodge was still the Balsam Grove Resort, owned and operated by the folks who built the place, Carl and Alis Brandt.

My father, Otto Nelson, was looked upon as the trail boss and organizer for all forms of hunting events. He put together some parties of well-known people, and with him they eagerly set off duck hunting in Saskatchewan, pheasant hunting in South Dakota or deer hunting in northern Minnesota.

On this particular occasion, a few of the notables included Freeborn County treasurer, Wilfred Knutson, Midway Motor Company owner, Art Jensen, and former world wrestling champion and senator, Helmer Myre, for whom the state park is named. Deer season in those years spanned Thanksgiving, and on that occasion the evening meal in the lodge was a very special turkey with all the trimmings.

The first wave of hungry hunters had left their cabins for the lodge when Helmer Myre suggested to Art Jensen and me that we could upstage the group of eager beavers by wearing ties to dinner. Art and Helmer had worn ties on the trip to the trail, but I hadn't. Somewhat reluctantly, I secured an odd looking one from a hook in an adjacent room and joined the others, even though I was wearing one of those black and red woolen hunting shirts.

Even though we received a few snickers and snide remarks when we entered the lodge, all seemed to be going well until Helmer rose to carve the turkey. Only a couple of slices into the bird, Helmer's son-in-law, Wilfred Knutson, rose from his chair across the table and announced that ties in the north woods were totally out of order. He drew his razor-sharp knife from its sheath, turned to Art Jensen, and slashed his two tie pendants just below the knot.

Cheers and laughter followed Wilfred as he walked to the end of the table, where a somewhat bewildered Helmer Myre had interrupted his turkey carving to watch his son-in-law go berserk. But with no hesitation, Wilfred lopped both pendants off Helmer's tie just below the knot.

My table position was well down the wall side, but a determined Wilfred, now laughing like crazy, worked his way past each chair. When he got to me and poised to make the final cut, his laughter ceased as he said, "Oh my God. That's my tie!" I, the one reluctant to wear any tie, especially this ugly one, was the only one left with a full-length tie for the rest of the dinner hour.

It is a bit difficult to pen for the record this lasting memory of that occasion because I, for quite a few years now, am the only surviving participant of that party. I remember very few hunting stories told at many game feeds held in the following years that surpassed this one. At Alis Brandt's 103rd birthday party a few years ago, she introduced me to her dozens of party guests as the only hunter who wore a full length tie to one of her Thanksgiving dinners at the lodge.

Near the Gunflint Trail, this is a panoramic shot of the inside of the Nor'wester Lodge, formerly the Balsam Grove Resort, where this story took place

The Nettle Patch
By Alice Stielow

It was a well known fact that Francie and I didn't want our sister Dolores butting into our time for playing, but one time her butting-in turned out to be more than a nuisance. One nice, warm summer day, Francie and I were going to take advantage of Mother and Daddy being gone for the day. We knew we had to play fast as they would be home in time for chores that evening.

We talked about how we should spend the afternoon, and our favorite game was to swing in the trees like monkeys. We went to the end of the grove and climbed our favorite tree, a big old willow, and decided that would be our starting point. The game was to see which one of us could get to the other end of the grove without falling out of a tree or touching the ground.

We were off like the devil was chasing us, our arms outstretched in a swimming motion, catching tree limbs as deftly as the monkeys we were trying to mimic. Now it was a neck and neck race; first I would be a few feet ahead, and then I lost time by missing one of the branches and almost falling to the ground. "Not quite," I yelled as I scrambled back to another branch that was a bit stronger.

I could hear branches cracking as we continued, branch over branch. Now just as Francie was getting ahead and my arms were getting tired, a big sharp branch poked a hole in my arm, with a little trickle of blood running off my elbow. I lost my grip and landed on the ground with a thump. "Ouch," I screamed, and Francie quickly came to my side, wondering if I was really hurt from the fall and where the blood was coming from.

We checked the hole in my arm, and it wasn't very big, but we decided we better go in and at least wash it and put a bandage on until Mother and Daddy came home, and then a long sleeved shirt would cover it up for a day or two. It would be hard to explain how I got poked with a sharp stick so it was just as good not to mention it.

Going to the house wasn't the right thing to do because Dolores wanted to come out and play with us for a little while, as she had the little kids taking a nap in the house. We couldn't think of a good reason she shouldn't play with us, but we did decide we would run away from her as soon as we could. We played hide and seek for a little while, and of course she was "it" and had to do the finding. Francie and I knew every inch of the yard and grove so we didn't have a hard time avoiding her. Finally we became bored because she just couldn't find us, so we went back up to the house, only to find she had quit looking and had gone back inside the house.

She took her time making sure all was well in the house. The little kids were still taking naps, and all was quiet. She said she would try to find us once more. Out we went again, she started counting to ten, and when she hollered, "Coming, ready or not," we weren't ready because we couldn't decide where would be the best hiding place. We heard her coming and of course she saw us, but she didn't tag either one of us. We were still safe so we took off around the house. Behind the house was a cesspool used for emptying the bathroom and kitchen water. It had an open dug drain that water spilled into when it overflowed. We knew we didn't want to run through the muck so Francie went to the left and I went to the right. Dolores didn't have the know-how that we had about bushes and trees, so what did she do but blast right down the middle, first hitting some muck, and then dashing through the nettle patch that we had taken care to avoid. Stinging nettle is a herb with little hairs on it. If you bump the little hairs, they give off an acid that stings like crazy.

We heard the loudest piercing scream, and it seemed that the sound sure couldn't have come from that little body that was chasing us. We knew in an instant just what had happened. Nothing but the nettle patch could bring on a scream like that. We dashed back to find her screaming and running in circles hollering, "What was that? What did I get into?" Francie and I knew just what a couple little spots of nettle felt like, but had no idea what Dolores must have been feeling at that minute.

When we grabbed her and started dragging her to the house, her little legs just couldn't keep up, and she slid along behind us screaming at the top of her voice all the way. After entering the house and dashing to the bathroom, we thought our best plan was to quickly get her into the bathtub soaking in cool water. Just like peeling a banana we stripped off her clothes and popped her into the tub of cool water. Still screaming, she said, "See what you did to me?" By now we were feeling pretty terrible as we watched big red welts spreading over her arms, legs and face. The screams stopped, but dirty tears ran down her face, and the screaming started coming from the other room where the little ones stood after being awakened from their naps. Boy oh boy, what had we done?

After she cooled for some time in the water, we got her out, dried her ever so carefully, and found some clean clothes for her to put on. By this time she was really mad at us and threatened to tell Mother what we had done if we didn't take care of the little ones for the rest of the afternoon. We did that without even arguing, while she sat on the chair giving orders: change Billy's diapers, get some crackers for them for lunch, make sure to only fill the milk glasses half full, and I know she had to be thinking up extras just to see what we would say.

The worst was last to come. We had to wash the dirty diapers that had been waiting for her to rinse out. Not a complaint did we make as she ordered us around like servants. Little did we know, but Mother would find out about it anyway as Dolores was still full of welts when she came home. Of course we got a good talking to, but we said we didn't know she would run through the nettle patch. Well, I guess they kind of believed us as it was then chores time, and we had to go to the barn and start feeding.

After the feeding was done I had to go to the house and help Dolores with the supper, and that was just as bad as getting bawled out. Back then I didn't like to be in the house, say nothing of helping with the cooking. I peeled some potatoes, got a jar of meat from the dark basement, where I knew the boogyman would be waiting to grab me just as I got to the stairway. I forgot the jar of vegetables so had to make the second trip. Just as I returned with the vegetables, Delores said, "Oh there is already a jar of them on the pantry shelf." Now I knew she was really getting even with me, but I didn't care because she looked like she had a bad case of measles or chicken pox.

Setting the table was another chore. I didn't do it right, and she kept telling me just where every dish and piece of silverware was to go. She tried to get me to make another trip to the basement for a jar of pickles, but I was smart enough to look in the pantry first, and sure enough there stood a jar of dills just waiting to be put into a dish. Supper over, dishes done, Mother told us to go up to bed and think about what we had done. Darn, to this day I really don't know what we did wrong. As far as Francie and I were concerned, Dolores was trying to ruin out afternoon of play time when she slipped into the nettle patch.

To this day Dolores has to keep busy all the time, but I guess we all inherited that from Daddy. She didn't usually have time to play back then because she was working in the house all the time and helping take care of all the little ones, and that was a never ending job. I think there must have been seven of us then. Dolores was the glue that held us all together, and I bless her for being there for us. Now that all three of us are in our mid to late 70s, I doubt that we will be running through the nettle patch again. Not in this life anyway, and I know in the next life there won't be any. The Lord won't have it.

Alice, Dolores and Francie Nilson, the nettle patch kids

Alice Stielow and her husband Richard have lived on the same farm near Clinton for almost 60 years. They have five daughters, one son and many grandchildren and great grandchildren. Over the years they have had one hundred foster children.

Fighting Fire
By Esther Haraldson

"Fire" was a word that would bring our family quickly into action on our 80-acre farm near Brook Park in Pine County. A potato farmer lived to the south of us, and in the spring he would burn off his fields. The railway line between Minneapolis and Duluth bordered our farm on the east. Between those two, we were vulnerable to fires during dry weather. The fire would start either from the burning off of the old potato fields or by a spark from the coal burning engines that traveled the rail lines in those days.

There were no fire departments in the small towns nearby so we would check the speed of distant smoke, gauge the wind direction and check to see if the fire causing the smoke appeared to be dangerous. If so, we would grab pails of water and old gunnysacks or rugs, along with our shovels and set off to control the approaching flames. We would set fire in the pasture and let that burn a barren strip for a firebreak. Then we'd use the water-soaked rugs or gunnysacks to put out the flames. Usually the firebreak would stop the encroaching wildfire.

One day I was the only one home with Mom and Dad, and the approaching fire was quickly burning into our fields. We drove the old truck over the pasture to get into the area were we could set a backfire. As we set to work, I was wetting down bags and putting out the flames.

Suddenly I heard my parents yell, "Esther, watch out for the fire!" I looked up and saw an approaching dust devil that had been stirred up by an especially erratic wind. Usually these little whirlwinds are harmless, but this dust devil was filled with flame. It was headed right for me and formidable enough so that no little wet burlap bag was going to quench its fire. My feet took wings. I wasn't too far from the swampy area so I headed at a dead run for that direction. I jumped over the fence in one flying leap and dove into the swamp.

As I stood in the mucky swamp, I turned around to view the enemy, but it had disappeared. As quickly as it had formed, it had disappeared. I stood ankle deep, panting in cold slime and breathed a prayer of thanks. I had no desire to be engulfed by that small tornado of fire.

Mother and Dad were also relieved, and our firebreak successfully stopped the encroaching flames. We were tired and sooty but happy that once more our farm home was safe.

This experience has helped me in life. Emotionally we also experience wildfires in our lives. So many times I've nearly been burned out by worry over what has seemed to be a threat to my well being. However, confident prayer and trust in knowing that God is still there and available to me has proven to be the necessary backfire to stop the panic.

Esther Haraldson on her family farm in Pine County

Esther Haraldson grew up near Brook Park, worked as a copywriter for radio stations in Iowa and South Dakota and wrote columns for the Aurora, MN newspaper. The wife of a minister, she has lived in many Midwest communities. She now lives in Shoreview and enjoys writing.

The Sting of Honey
By Esther Haraldson

Hot weather reminds me of the pleasure I had as a girl, walking down our half-mile sandy Pine County road to our rural mailbox on a hot summer day. I was usually barefoot all summer, and the sand always felt cool on my feet by contrast. We had one low spot in our road, swampy on both sides, where our car invariably got stuck every spring. Willows grew there, and Dad could make the best whistles from their branches, as the bark easily slipped off the wood. As I walked the path, it was especially cool in the shade of those willows.

As I became older I was able to fetch the mail in less time by riding my bike. Sometimes I really flew down the path, and on one particular day I set a world record for speed. The neighbor who lived along the road was a fellow who kept bees as a hobby, and one day they took after me. I was pedaling as fast as I could with that huge cloud of bees swarming right behind me. Mom said it was my red sweater that attracted them. Much to my relief, the bees became distracted before they caught up to me.

One year those bees flew all the way over to our house and swarmed under our wooden siding. When we became aware that our wall was buzzing, we called the neighbor, and he came over to claim his bees. He wore a head covering and carried a smoker, a device he used to temporarily pacify the bees with smoke before invading their nest. Sensing danger from the smoke, worker bees gorge themselves with honey and become sluggish for a while.

Getting rid of the bees was not an easy task. We had to rip part of our siding off to destroy the nest. The man gave us several nice combs of honey, and his bees left us to return to his place, so all that work was worth the effort. I've always preferred comb honey since that time I tasted it for the first time.

Most difficult things turn out to be worth the effort, although that effort might prove challenging and even frustrating. When we accept the fact that life will sometimes be hard, that's when life becomes easier.

It All Started in My Bedroom
By Gloria Wilkinson

During World War II, I attended college in Winona, in the southeast corner of the state. My father lived in Oklee, in northern Minnesota, as a railroad agent for the Soo Line Railroad. One of his job perks was free passes on the train for his family and himself. Therefore, wherever we went, we went by train.

During my college years I traveled back and forth between Winona and Oklee, changing trains in Minneapolis. Many GIs traveled by train during those years, and what a uniform did for a guy! They were all close to my age so I got into many lively conversations, and a good time was had by all. The conductor took it all in stride and just said, "Just remember to get off where you're supposed to. This locomotive does not go in reverse."

After graduation I accepted a teaching position in the small town of Parkers Prairie in west central Minnesota near Alexandria. I traveled there by train, of course, arriving very tired at 5 a.m. In those days people traveled with a trunk, and everything I owned was in my trunk. There were no apartments so single teachers rented rooms in private homes. I had my own bedroom but shared the family bathroom and ate at restaurants. My landlady's son met me at the train and said he would hire a friend to bring my trunk later.

I immediately put on my shorty pajamas and went to bed. At 6:30 my landlady knocked at my door to tell me that she had to go somewhere but that I should make myself at home. I rolled over and went back to sleep. At 8:30 another knock woke me. I thought, "Here she is again," so half asleep, I crawled out of bed to answer the door.

I was so surprised and embarrassed that I almost fainted when I opened the door. There stood a nice young man. He said, "I'm here to deliver your trunk."

Proper young ladies were not supposed allow gentlemen into their bedrooms. Caught by surprise, I just stood there in my little jammies and said, "Bring it in," which he did, and then he turned to leave.

Trying my hardest to think of something to say besides thank you, I said, "Is there a restaurant nearby where I can have breakfast?"

And just like in the movies he said, "Well, I'm going for coffee in about an hour. I can come and get you and show you where it is. By the way, my name is Bill. See you in about an hour, if that's okay."

He came back, we went out and the rest is history. We were married fifty-seven years and had three sons. It all started in my bedroom. And I still have that trunk.

Gloria, the new teacher in town

Gloria Wilkinson taught for twenty years in Underwood. She has ten grandchildren and ten great-grandchildren. After her husband William died in 2004, she started a club for widows at Our Lady of Victory Church in Fergus Falls. The one rule is that you can't talk about your ailments.

Serving Mass on Christmas Eve in 1943
By Robert Walsh

Our country was fighting a dreadful war that Christmas of 1943, and it had been a cold, dark winter, but in our little town we made a supreme effort to create a little peace, light, warmth and beauty. My brothers Dick, Jack and I were serving midnight mass at Sacred Heart Church in Belle Plaine, so we had to be at church a little early.

We walked five blocks to church in the bright moonlight, hurrying along in the cold. When we arrived, we put on our outfits. Dick and Jack were regular altar boys, so they each wore a long red cassock with a white surplice over the top. I was just a little guy, but I had the same thing plus a little red shawl over my shoulders. All I was supposed to do was carry a lighted candle and stand in a row with the other little guys, Lee Lynch, Lee Engfer, Jerry Doheny, Jim Ciminski and Roger Hessian.

Earlier in the week, Mom and other parish ladies had washed and ironed the cassocks and surplices, cleaned and polished the brass candlesticks and the altar. They put on fresh altar cloths that were washed, starched and ironed to a crisp, clean finish. The sanctuary floor had a fresh coat of wax and glowed with the luster of good wood. The altar and communion railing had been dusted, and the marble top was gleaming. The crèche was placed in front of Saint Joseph's statue, and someone had cut trees and set them up around and behind it.

The parish was making Christmas as bright as it could in that dark time. Father Farrell, a large, imposing man with a magnificent voice, had us practice several times during the week so we all knew what to do. We lined up all our candle holders and lit the candles. The candlesticks were wood with brass trim on top and bottom, about three feet high, and the candles were a foot long. There were six bigger guys plus Dick and Jack who went out and lit the candles on the altar.

For high mass, they lit the six high candles, three on either side of the tabernacle, that were about three feet tall and stood in three-foot high candlesticks. For Christmas they also lit the lower candles in brass candlesticks about two feet tall. Along each side of the altar stood candle holders with a cross arm at the top and seven candles on each arm.

People filed into the church in great numbers. Dad came in and sat with my sisters Alice, Rose and baby Sis, and Mom sat up in the choir loft. Mother had a beautiful voice that could ring out loud and clear. We all lined up as midnight arrived, and the choir was singing a carol. When it ended, the lead boy rang a small brass bell, and we went out into the sanctuary. The choir was singing, the organ was playing, all the lights were turned on and all the candles were lit. We boys were dressed in red and white, and Father Farrell wore his white and gold vestments. It was beautiful, overwhelmingly beautiful!

Of course, the mass was sung in Latin. Younger people today have missed a thing of beauty by not hearing the Gloria and all the other parts sung in Latin by a choir and a good priest leader. The church didn't have any audio equipment in those days, but it didn't matter. The church was filled with God and angels, good people and good music—It was wonderful. When Mass was over, we took our candles and filed into the sacristy. We blew the candles out, put the other stuff away, and got ready to go home. Before we left, we got holy cards from Father and knelt for his blessing. As we walked home in the cold night air, the Northern Lights were dancing in the heavens, and that was awesome.

When we got home, Dad was frying bacon and eggs so we had an early-morning breakfast. Then we opened gifts because Santa had come while we were gone. We knew better, but it was fun to go along with it!

Church of the Sacred Heart in Belle Plaine,

Robert Walsh lives in Cannon Falls. The Church of the Sacred Heart has been torn down, and the parish merged with St. Peter and Paul to become a new parish, Our Lady of the Prairie Church and School.

Unplanned Family Reunion at the Lake
By Michael Harvey

One summer in the early 1950s, Mom made plans to spend a few days at a lake near Pelican Rapids with my sister Joan and me. No one else, only the three of us. We all looked forward to the trip. Although we lived only a few steps west of Minnesota in Grand Forks, we usually spent vacation time near the Canada border in Walhalla, North Dakota. We went there for Christmas, Easter, Thanksgiving, Fourth of July, birthdays or because Grandma Mathison decided we must all be together.

Two days before the scheduled departure for our three-person Minnesota vacation, the phone rang. Grandma called to announce a visit. Uncle Allan planned to drive her and Grandpa down and go right back to Walhalla. Grandma asked if Mom needed more potatoes. Uncle Allan worked in a potato warehouse as an inspector. Periodically he brought Mom a hundred-pound sack of really good potatoes. He handpicked them as the nicest ones in the warehouse.

Rats! Darn! Dang it! Mom asked Grandma to please wait before coming to Grand Forks, as we would not be home. Grandma, of course, asked where-on-earth we planned to be, if not at home. When Mom revealed our plans for staying at the cabin near Pelican Rapids for a few quiet days, Grandma got excited.

Her sisters lived close to the lake, not too far from other members of her family. Mom wasn't to worry, Grandma would take care of starting the family telephone tree. Grandma made one long distance call to her sister Sina. Sina called their sister Ida. Once those three Thompson sisters knew something, it spread around the world like a wildfire–at least around our portion of the world.

Somehow Mom, Joan and I became part of a five-person expedition. I don't think Mom got to say a word after her mother heard about the cabin. Uncle Allan brought his parents and the potatoes, which he put in Mom's trunk. Potatoes in the trunk, we started off to the lake, with Grandpa in the front passenger seat, Mom driving, and poor Joan trapped between Grandma and me in the back seat.

As soon as we arrived at the lake, everything was unpacked, except for the potatoes. Grandma opened the bag and took out a few for supper. Each cabin came equipped with a small rowboat. Grandpa went to the other rented cabins and explained why we'd like to use the boat that came with their cabin on Sunday. With all of the relatives scheduled to be there, we required a lot of boats. Of course, Grandpa also invited all of the cabin renters who lent us their boats to come to the Sunday fish fry as compensation for the use of their boats.

Grandpa was persuasive, and soon a half-dozen vacationers promised the use of their boats for Sunday. He also talked to the resort owner and got permission for us to use any boats that didn't get rented out as part of a vacation package deal. Several relatives planned to trailer in their own boats.

With a hundred pounds of potatoes, ten pounds of flour, three dozen raw eggs and several bottles of fresh milk, everything was in place. Grandma went around to the women in the other cabins and asked to borrow their frying pans and spatulas for the Sunday gala. Mom did not appear to be enjoying the vacation as much as her bustling parents.

Sure enough, Sunday became bedlam. Women worked in the hot kitchen, cooking potatoes by the potful, to be ready for the fish fry. Men and kids spent the day in boats fishing, with queasy kids getting seasick. Seasick kids got rowed to shore and banned from ever going out in any boat again. Kids who threw up inside the boats, instead of over the side, most likely got banned from growing up.

As they caught the first fish, fishermen rowed to shore, to give the cooks a head start. The fish-cleaning house became a scene of constant turmoil. Queasy kids soon were banished from there as well–for the same reason they got banned from the boats or from growing up. Soon every burner held a pan, full of frying fish.

When the cooks lagged behind, because of lack of space on the stove, Grandma sent cooking parties to scout out nearby cabins for stoves not in use. Mom counted over one hundred and fifteen relatives moving through our cabin that day. That does not include the neighbors from nearby cabins eating fish, to make up for their borrowed boats.

It is possible that someone stood out on the paved road, waving perfect strangers in for the big fish fry. As with most gatherings of this nature, there was a ton of food left over. Everyone took home a bunch of fried fish and mashed potatoes.

With the last plate dried and either put away or returned to a beleaguered neighbor, Mom looked exhausted. In addition to all of the preceding chaos, the toilet plugged up — twice. Queasy kids finally got banned from everywhere, except deep in the piney woods.

On our next family vacation, Mom called Grandma from Fargo, after we'd been gone from home for over an hour.

Michael Harvey's grandmother with all her siblings and their husbands.

*Michael Harvey lives in Grand Forks, North Dakota, where his home is a regular gathering place for writers, film makers and others who have a story to tell. His story, "The Best Gift of All" appears in **The Rocking Chair Reader-Family Gatherings**.   MMHarvey@hotmail.com*

Tunney
By Janet Anhorn Gaughran

It was 1926 when my father, Art Anhorn, brought home a new puppy, a three-quarter bulldog/terrier, whom he promptly named Tunney after the world's heavyweight champion boxer of 1926, Gene Tunney. Tunney would turn out to be no ordinary bulldog. By 1928 he had become the protector of Art and Mildred's oldest son, Donnie. Still in rompers, Donnie had only to stray a little outside of their large backyard on Maple Street, and Tunney would grab Donnie from behind by his diapers and gently pull him back to the safety of the yard.

When he got a little older, Tunney became known to all the townsfolk as the Pure Oil dog who rode on the running board of Art's company pickup truck. If Art went around the corner too fast, Tunney often tumbled off, but he always came running to jump back on the running board.

Art Anhorn, along with his cousins from Owatonna, Andrew and John Anhorn, had founded the Mower County Oil Company in Austin in 1922, selling Pure Oil products. The company opened on Brownsdale Avenue, which became their bulk plant near the railroad tracks. In 1925 the company expanded and opened the uptown station at Main and Oakland. A third station opened on Water Street, along with eight other outlets.

Tunney liked to make the rounds each day of all the Pure Oil stations in Austin. Because doing that would involve a lot of walking, Tunney made friends with all the bus drivers in the city. Tunney had merely to go to a bus stop and wait until the bus came along. The driver would stop and open the door for him, and Tunney would ride to the next station, where the driver would let him out. As the townspeople came to know Tunney, they would often stop for him as well when they spotted him waiting at the curb.

Using his personality and intelligence, Tunney soon made friends with the pilots as well at the Austin Airport. They were also generous with their rides, and Tunney came to love flying. At the gas stations, Tunney again showed his protective behavior. He placed himself at the station's entrance, and if a man showed up who was ragged or smelly, Tunney would not let him enter the station door.

At 11 years of age, Tunney was proposed for membership in the Old Timer's Club by a group of dealers from the Mower County Oil Company. Tunney also became their official mascot, and was present at all of their dealer meetings.

Tunney lived a long and useful life. He will always be remembered as the Pure Oil dog who was named after the famous boxer of his time. Like Gene Tunney, he was a champion as well. Well known to the townspeople of Austin, he captured many of their hearts. Tunney was much more than a dog; Tunney was a person.

Donnie Anhorn and the amazing Tunney at their home in Austin

*Janet Anhorn Gaughan lives in Jordan. This story was first featured in the book **Austin Remembers**, published in 2006 by the Friends of the Austin Public Library*

The Klan
By Mary Kalkes James

Wall Street crashed in 1929, but on our farm near Northfield we did not feel the full effects until a year or so later when farm prices started to fall steeply. By then we were in a drought cycle, a time sometimes known as the dust bowl or the dirty thirties. By June our pastures were brown, and we had to cut young corn to feed our cattle.

Just prior to this discouraging time, Ku Klux Klansmen had come up from the South to Minnesota. They held rallies near small towns, trying to enlist and organize white, Protestant men to join the Klan. Since we did not have any racial minorities to hate, their bigotry focused on Catholics. They opposed Al Smith, a Catholic who ran for president in 1928, and after that they blamed the economy on the Pope and the Catholic Church. Their presence in the Northfield area gave a little excitement to some people's dull lives in those days before television, radio or telephones in most farmhouses. Nobody had money for other forms of entertainment.

I have a clipping from the *Northfield News* that states that an estimated 400 sheeted Klansmen paraded down the main street of town one Saturday night. The Klan burned crosses at night in front of the Catholic church, and we had a new Catholic school staffed by four nuns from Mankato. The very first night they were in town, someone burned a cross on their convent lawn, terrifying them.

Our hired man would walk into town Saturday nights, and on Sunday he would tell us the news at the breakfast table. He would tell how this neighbor or that one had joined the Klan. He said that one neighbor said he wasn't going to exchange threshing help with my father, Gus Kalkes, because we were Catholics. Since we were the only Catholics on our road, I think my parents were worried, but they didn't let on.

As summer got hotter and dryer, the relentless weather stunted our crops. My father decided to stack our grain because to do that you didn't need as large a crew. If you left the shocks in the field, you needed twelve to fourteen helpers. If you stacked, you could get by with about eight. My father did not put all his stacks in one area. He put maybe ten or twelve together and then made more across the field to protect the grain. In case of lightning or some other disaster, there was a chance that not all would be destroyed. One hot morning I brought lunch out to the field and was playing with the dog in the shade of the stacks when a pickup came racing across the field, throwing up clouds of dust. It was our good neighbor Fred Gongolus, and his son. They pulled up and shouted, "Fred Chester's field is on fire!" And then they drove off.

Fred's farm was about a mile and a half from ours, and he was one of the neighbors who had joined the Klan. My father climbed down the ladder and told the hired man to unhitch the team and take it to the barn. He and Eddie, the young man my parents had raised, climbed into the truck that was by the stack. They drove to the shop and took shovels, sacks and cans of water, and with the hired man went to the fire. Fred Chester had put all his stacks together up near his barn. When my father, Eddie and the hired man arrived, Fred was frantically plowing between the stacks and the fire, which was running in the stubble field. There was a swamp a good ways away that had peat in it. During the long drought the swamp had gone dry, and somehow the peat had caught fire. It may have been smoldering for days before wind blew it right into the field.

Other neighbors arrived, and then more. They beat out the flames with wet sacks and shoveled dirt onto the fire. The work was exhausting. Sometimes the fire seemed to be out, and then it would break out again, but finally it was extinguished. The men stood around all soaked with sweat, their faces and eyebrows singed. My father's straw hat brim was charred as he looked around the circle of neighbors. That was when something good happened.

Fred Chester stood in the center of the group, thanking everyone for saving his crop. Then he made a little speech. He said, "I want you all to know that I will never go to another Klan meeting. When I needed help, the first man here was Gus Kalkes."

Some of the others looked down and shifted their feet. Nobody else spoke up or said anything to either agree or disagree, but that was pretty much the end of the Klan in our neighborhood. A year later it had died out everywhere in the area.

Florida resident Mary Kalkes James is 92 years old. During summers she comes back to her hometown, Northfield.

The Green Parking Lot
By Dave Healy

Fly over any town in America, and from the air one of the landscape's most obvious features is the number of baseball diamonds. Rare is the school or park or playground that doesn't have at least one backstop and demarcated infield. It's common these days to read that football has supplanted baseball, our first love, in the hearts and minds of Americans, but judging strictly by the number of playing fields across the country, the contest—if there is one—isn't even close. Nearly every citizen—rural, small town, or urban—ends up spending some time on a baseball or softball field—a claim no other sport can match.

Most baseball fields are put in place deliberately. Though they vary considerably in sophistication and amenities, they share a certain intentionality. Occasionally, however, a field that never existed in any set of blueprints will evolve because a need emerges, in the same way a path will develop between two points even though no architect or landscape engineer planned one there. Such was the case with The Green.

"The Green" has a bit of a poetic or aristocratic ring to it. It doesn't sound like the sort of name that a bunch of kids would give to a baseball field, and indeed the genesis was not ours. Actually, Green was our shorthand for the oxymoronic Green Parking Lot on the Minnesota State Fairgrounds. With huge shopping malls a fixture on the urban landscape, it's become common for parking lots to have names—a convenience for dazed shoppers who might otherwise forget where they left the car. In the pre-mall 1960s, however, parking lot names were unnecessary—except at the State Fairgrounds. And fair officials, who didn't have to compete with the Panda Lot or the Gnu Lot or the Ferrari Lot or the Sopwith Camel Lot, could afford to keep things simple: Green, Yellow, Red, Blue.

The designation of the fairground's other lots was pretty arbitrary, but the Green's moniker seemed to make sense, for in addition to the usual blacktop, the Green Parking Lot included a large grassy area that was reserved for the fair's tent and trailer crowd. This part of the fairgrounds was the first to fill up every August. It housed people who came for the whole shebang—exhibitors mostly—and their Airstreams and Winnebagos began showing up before the State Fair even started.

During June, July, and the first half of August though, the Green Parking Lot was our turf, and a baseball game took place nearly every day. All of us who played at the Green lived within three or four blocks of the field. But to even call it a "field" is to get slightly ahead of things, for it was simply a large open area bounded by a chain link fence on two sides, a street on the third, and several acres of asphalt on the fourth.

One of the fences ran along Snelling Avenue and was topped with barbed wire, designed to keep kids like us from sneaking into the fair. Simple expediency dictated that our field not be too close to the fence, since a ball hit over it would oblige someone to run back down to the gate and then do battle with traffic on Snelling. We laid out the bases so that this fence was well out of play, while the other one, which ran perpendicular to it, served as a left field wall. This was a fairly serviceable arrangement, although it left us without a backstop—a considerable liability, given the quality of the average tenant behind the plate.

Without a backstop, no one who walked by the Green when we weren't playing would have recognized it as a baseball field—at least to start with. Eventually, the infield took on some definition as the bases, pitcher's mound, and home plate area wore away. In time, a baseball field emerged, and the Green Parking Lot assumed an alter ego. "If you build it," the voice said to Ray Kinsella, "he will come." For us, the coming came first, and building it was simply a matter of working with the terrain at hand. Ray Kinsella in *Field of Dreams* turned useful land into a useless ballpark that was the scorn of his neighbors. We took land that lay fallow for eleven months of the year and gave it another purpose.

For the first year or two that we played at the Green, the fence in left field never came into play because none of us could reach it. As we got older though, it became a tempting target, and right-handed pull hitters multiplied. The only problem was that this fence separated the Green Parking Lot from the back yard of a house. There were three houses on the fairgrounds, all occupied year-round by maintenance personnel and their families. This one was a regular two-story stucco affair that looked just like the ones we lived in a few blocks away, except that instead of being surrounded by other similar houses, it sat there by itself, within a stone's throw of the big silo near Machinery Hill.

We knew that people lived in this house, but we rarely saw them. For that reason, the house acquired a sense of mystery. What sort of people would actually live on the fairgrounds all year? What did they do from September through July? More important, what did they do during State Fair time? If they went to the grocery store, did they have to pay to get back in when they came home? Maybe they were stuck there for the whole ten days—a fate we contemplated enviously.

Home runs to left, even after several us grew strong enough to reach the fence, remained a rarity and were accompanied by equal parts jubilation and dread. After the offensive team's celebration, someone, presumably the left fielder, would have to go around to the gate, dash into the yard, and retrieve the ball. I'm not sure why this prospect was so foreboding. Perhaps we were afraid that one of the house's occupants would kick us off the field. The status of the Green Parking Lot was hazy enough in our minds that our daily presence there during the summer always seemed a bit anomalous. It wasn't designed as a baseball field, after all. It was a parking lot. We weren't even sure who owned it. Who does own the fairgrounds anyway?

The kind of baseball we played was typical sandlot ball, which is to say that we spent as much time arguing as we did playing. There was inexhaustible fodder for arguments: who should be captains, were we going to play pitcher's-hands-out, did teams have to supply their own catcher, was the power line that ran from right field to center field in play, could you switch from batting right-handed to left-handed in the same at-bat, what kind of compensation should Danny Olson's team get when he had to leave (as he invariably did) before the game was over, could Mark McTie be called out when he had refused to swing at ten consecutive two-strike pitches, was Dave Eardley's 38-inch bat legal, and so on. Some of these issues were necessarily ongoing, depending on who showed up to play on a given day, but most of them could simply have been decided once and for all. For some reason, though, we preferred to debate them on a daily basis.

One day, in the throes of one of these disputes, Tommy Nace paused suddenly in the middle of an eloquent and passionate exegesis of the infield fly rule. "Somebody's coming." We followed his gaze. A man got out of a green Minnesota State Fair truck and began walking purposefully toward the field. "That's the guy who lives in the house." So, we figured, it's all over. We should have known. Who did we think we were, playing baseball in the fairgrounds? What were we trying to do, wreck this spot? Didn't we know it was used during the fair? How did we get across Snelling Avenue? Did our parents know we were here?

The man stopped next to home plate. "I've seen you guys over here a lot." Silence. Here it comes. Billy Nace was already edging toward the gate. "I've got a son who's about the same age as you guys. We live right over there." He pointed at the stucco house. "I was wondering if you'd let him play ball with you."

Whiff. We were ready for a fast one, high and tight, and instead we got a breaking pitch, low and away. "His name's Mark. He's got a really nice bat and a whole bag full of balls." Now what? We didn't really have a spokesman. If we had, we probably wouldn't have spent so much time arguing. Ours was a meritocracy, but the merit was spread thinly enough so that no clear leader had ever emerged. Usually that wasn't much of a problem. Unlike football, baseball doesn't particularly need leaders. But in the face of this question, our leadership vacuum collapsed us.

It wasn't as though there was much of anything to debate. We knew we were on somebody else's property. This guy lived and worked there, so obviously he was in a position to kick us out. He hadn't done it yet, but we all sensed the implied threat—intentional or not—behind his question. So it was just a matter of somebody playing out the script. Finally, Danny Olson stepped into the breach.

"Sure, that'd be great. What's your son's name?"

The rest of us cringed at this staged enthusiasm, but the man seemed satisfied. "Mark," he replied. "Mark Fischler."

As if on cue, a figure emerged from the green truck and approached the field. "Here he is. Hey Mark, these guys want you to play ball with them." Danny's slightly over-dramatized reply notwithstanding, this wasn't exactly what we had said, but nobody was about to press our luck at that point. So we waited for Mark to make a move. But he just stood there next to his dad.

"Well, I've got work to do," said Mr. Fischler. "Have a good time." With that he walked back to his truck. We stood and looked at Mark.

"You guys can have him," said Dave Eardley. Ordinarily this attempted transaction would have been grist for at least ten minutes of argument, but no one challenged Eardley.

"Okay," said Tommy Nace. Then to Mark, "You're up last."

The rest of the game passed uneventfully. Mark Fischler proved to be about what you'd expect in a ball player whose dad had to ask to get him in a game. His first time up he struck out, which meant that the next time he took a page from his namesake Mark McTie's book and watched ten perfectly good pitches go by before finally swinging and grounding weakly to second. In the field he stated his desire to pitch but was roundly ignored, so he grudgingly trotted out to right field, where he managed to lose a fly ball in the sun and then throw wildly past second, allowing the runner to go to third. The game ended with all of us in a funk.

That was Friday. We generally didn't play baseball over the weekend, and when we got to the Green on Monday, Mark Fischler was waiting for us. Something else was waiting too. A backstop had been constructed in what formerly was center field, effectively transposing the infield and outfield. Now the fence along Snelling ran from right field to center, the asphalt portion of the Green Parking Lot was in deep left field, and Mark Fischler's house was in foul territory, well out of play.

"Where'd that come from?" asked Billy Nace.

"My dad had it built," said Mark Fischler. "He supervises a whole bunch of guys, and they put it up in one day. Pretty nice, huh? The posts are set in concrete."

There was no doubt about it—this was an impressive backstop. The chain link looked brand new, and it was high enough to stop almost any foul ball we'd ever hit. Plus, without any catcher's gear or even a bona fide catcher, a backstop would be more than ornamental. So we accepted the new layout.

A game began. This time, Mark Fischler was involved from the beginning, which made his deficiencies all the more glaring. He couldn't catch or throw, he took forever to swing with two strikes, he wouldn't let anyone else use his bat. And he was whiny. When he couldn't pitch or bat leadoff, he complained. Somehow, without ever saying so directly, he managed to hint that his dad wouldn't be too happy if he found out his kid always had to play right field.

So, we acquiesced. We moved him up in the batting order and let him pitch once in a while. We still thought he was a jerk, but we knew who his old man was, and we knew we were squatters. "You do what you have to do," said Tommy Nace.

As I write these words, Minnesotans are in the grip of winter. All that keeps some of us going are thoughts of baseball and the knowledge that in a few months another generation of bat-and-ball-toting kids will seek out an Elysian field on which to enact the national pastime. They won't be playing at the Green Parking Lot. That area is now called the Rooster Lot. Our backstop has long since been torn down, and permanent hook-ups have been installed for trailers and mobile homes, rendering the area unfit for baseball. But there will be other fields. As another generation of urban pioneers scours the city, looking for an unused spot, Yankee ingenuity will rise to the occasion and a new field of dreams will emerge. I wonder if Mark Fischler's grandkid will be a ballplayer.

Dave Healy is a lifelong resident of St. Paul. Though his baseball career ended long ago, he still remains a fan. He is a freelance writer and editor, and lives with his wife, Nancy, in a recently emptied nest. He can be reached at dhealy@soncom.com.

Newcomer to a Small Town
By Carol Keech Malzahn

About the time many kids my age were testing their wings and flying away from the Maple River area, I was just arriving. To be exact, it was October 1974. I had applied, interviewed, and been offered a job with Nordaas American Homes (NAH) in Minnesota Lake, as a secretary/tour girl. As I drove my dad's two-toned, Buick Omega east on Highway 30 from the rural St. James area, I thought, "How many times do you think I will be making this trip in the coming years?"

Passing through the fair city of Amboy, I speculated that perhaps I would meet a man and settle down here. When I stopped at the stop sign in Mapleton to turn south onto Highway 22, I never imagined my children would be graduating from the big brick high school on my left.

As I approached Minnesota Lake, I could barely believe my eyes. The huge Nordaas American Homes office building rose up to the sky like the White House itself. I had seen the White House the summer before during a week-long 4-H trip. Wow, I had finally stumbled onto some good luck in my nineteenth year on this earth. I could feel this was the place for me, and all things were looking bright.

Anxious to begin my new life in Minnesota Lake, I took up residence with the Ed and Thelma Evan family. Most of their children were grown, married and living in their own homes. The three youngest still lived at home. I could share a bedroom with Tut, aka, Theresa, and join the family for all their meals for $40 per month. Tut was also a tour girl at NAH. She had been assigned to show me around my first day at work. Tut's mom, Thelma, would do my laundry for an extra $5 a month if I wanted. The arrangement was perfect in my eyes. I was all moved in before the first snow fell.

One day, as I was ironing my shirt in Thelma's kitchen, a young man who was a stranger to me drove up the driveway, got out of his car and proceeded to walk right into the house and stand in front of me. He did not knock or ring the doorbell or ask if it was all right to come in. I stood there petrified, with that hot iron in my hand, plotting to use it for a weapon against this intruder. I was there alone. He began asking way too many questions. I believe I asked him to leave, but I was terrified and don't recall to this day exactly what conversation transpired between the two of us. I know he left after what seemed like forever. I later found out he was related to the Evans, totally harmless, and I had no reason to have been terrified.

"Oh we have people walking into our house all the time," Ed later chuckled at me. He had heard the entire story uptown before I even had a chance to tell any of the Evan family about my harrowing experience! I found out the next day at work, during coffee break, that EVERYONE in town had heard about my frightening experience. It was quite an embarrassment hearing more about it from my co-workers than I could even recall myself! I learned that I had struck quite a threatening pose, along with my hot iron, to this young man whom everyone in Minnesota Lake knew and apparently loved. So began the first of many embarrassing moments and stories I would become a part of in this small town life.

After a hard week of work at NAH, Friday night was *the* night to go directly uptown to the "muni." The legal drinking age at the time had been lowered to 18. The slogan of the day went something like this: "If our 18-year-olds are old enough to die fighting the war in Viet Nam, they should be old enough to drink alcohol legally."

Our boss and owner of the company, Haakon Nordaas, occasionally joined us at the muni. When he lifted his glass for a toast, we all courteously reciprocated the gesture – "No Problem, Skoal, Yah!" he would shout out in his thick, robust, Norwegian accent. Occasionally he would slap down a hundred dollar bill for us to buy drinks and food with for the night or he would leave word with the waitress, at the bar, that he would cover our tab. I was overwhelmed with the kindness and generosity of this community.

One Friday night as a group of us from NAH joined a few "town" gals already occupying the round booth in the corner at the muni, I took it upon myself to make the introductions. I knew these gals by now, and a couple of newly hired salesmen from the company had decided to join us. All in attendance politely gave me their attention as I began the introductions. I stuck with the basics, name and what department they worked in at NAH, until I came to the town gals. A couple of them were

Tut's sisters so that was a cinch. Then I came to Edie. "Edie More, this is Willy Bach," I spouted off in my all-knowing voice. Edie extended her hand to Willy.

Nordaas American Homes employed 33 people in Minnesota Lake.

"Glad to meet you. Did she say your name was Willy?" Willy nodded his head, as a smirk spread across his face. He politely stood to reach Edie's hand. Then he sat back with a big smile across his face. I further offered up how Willy was a salesman at NAH and Edie played softball against us "Nordaas Girls" on Tuesday nights, down at the park by the lake. One of the girls finally burst out in laughter. I quickly scoped out the group for an explanation. They were all laughing so hard no one could even tell me what the heck was so funny.

Anyone FROM Minnesota Lake knows that Willy Bach and Edie More are brother and sister! I later found out nearly everyone at that table was a first or second cousin, if not sibling, to everyone else. I quickly learned to keep my mouth shut and be more observant as a newcomer to the big city. You see, I did move to the "big city" of Minnesota Lake, population 650, from Sveadahl, population 15 (maybe). Minnesota Lake was in its heyday. The town was flourishing, and new people were moving in. I wasn't the newcomer for very long! Thank goodness.

Carol Malzahn, who still lives in Minnesota Lake, grew up on a farm near Sveadahl. She and her husband Art have two adult children.

Paperboy
By Carolyn Light Bell

Winter darkness isn't like summer darkness. Light inside houses is golden, like what a caterpillar sees in a milkweed pod. Home and family are closer than usual. When someone visits from the outside during a Minnesota winter, it's a big occasion because you know the person has suffered pain to get to your house.

I didn't know his name, but I liked the paperboy who came to collect at dinnertime. His arrival provided an escape from Mother's tiresome rules. She took her role as Keeper of Table Manner Standards very seriously and didn't trust we'd learn unless she repeated every rule: *Sit up straight! Elbows off the table! One hand in your lap! Don't reach for seconds! Ask politely!*

When the back doorbell buzzed, I was the first one out of my chair. "Paperboy!" I shouted. Father was close behind, eager to talk to any boy who worked hard. He liked that in a boy. When I turned on the porch light, steam haloed the boy's head. Two giant blue eyes, bright as the moon, lit up his frosty face. He was older than I was– 10 or 11. His nose dripped, and he wore his cap's fur-lined ear flaps up, with the strap hanging down so he could hear.

We examined each other from a distance. I stood watching for a long time and then remembered to open the door wider. "C'mon in." He stomped snow off his black buckle overshoes and rolled his red, chapped hands into fists, trying to warm them. I tried not to stare at the holes in the fingertips of his brown cotton gloves as he tore off the yellow receipt from a tablet. The squares were small as stamps and impossible to tear at the perforations without ripping off a ragged edge of one next to it.

Father wiped ketchup off his mouth. He paid his debt, jingled change, and flipped an extra dime off his thumb into the boy's outstretched palm. "Keep it, son. How 'bout a big piece of lemon meringue pie?"

Through chattering teeth, he said, "N-no thanks, s-sir, I've got a lot of houses ahead of me. Maybe next time. Thanks anyway."

He disappeared into the huge, starry night, and I stepped outside under the porch light watching him until I felt my lungs freeze. The next Wednesday, when the paperboy should have come, his father came instead, wearing the same fur-lined hat, strap buckled firmly under his chin. Father didn't invite him in, but I asked where his son was. "Sick," he answered, collected his money, and turned away. I didn't see the paperboy for the rest of the winter, and I heard lots of children in the neighborhood had gotten polio.

The following summer, I recognized the paperboy cutting through our driveway toward Lake Harriet, a fishing pole slung over his shoulder. Our long driveway started at the alley, spread out wide in front of the garage, and spilled sharply down the hill. All kids cut through yards or driveways on their way somewhere: to the store, to steal apples, or to go to the lake. The unwritten laws were: *Look like you know where you're going and make a break for it. Don't get caught because someone will ask you questions. If you get scratched on a bush or bitten by a dog, never cry out; just keep going.*

I was transfixed by the paperboy, but scared to approach. I wanted to know what was wrong, what kept him away from our route. One day, when I was cutting through the yard across the alley to get to my friend, Snake Princess' house, Mrs. King, who drank all day, stuck her head out the window, clutching the neck of her bathrobe. She shouted at me, "I'm calling your mother, you little heathen!" Her voice hurt my whole body.

I sat down in the alley, holding my head, trying to figure out how to maneuver around Mrs. King to keep from getting in trouble. Snake's mother was driving home through the alley. When she saw me, she slowed down, her tires spitting gravel, and rolled down her window to call out, "Did you fall, sweetheart? Are you all right?" She eased her car forward, toward me.

I tried to look casual as I jumped up out of the path of her car and brushed off the gravel. "Oh, yeah, I just tripped! I'm fine." She rolled her window back up and disappeared into her garage. Just at that moment, I saw the paperboy cutting through with his three-legged dog.

I caught up to him. "Hey, what's your dog's name?"

"Spike," he said, head down, resuming his loose-legged lope back toward my house and the lake. "He's not really mine. He just follows me. He likes me, I guess."

"How'd he lose his leg?" I tripped along next to him.

"Chasing streetcars." He stole a sidelong glance at me.

"That's too bad. Do you ever take the streetcar?"

"Yup.

"I love the streetcar. I go to the arena to skate. I love the smell of streetcars. They smell like giant magnets." I had a new friend. I wanted to show him the arena. "Were you very sick when you stopped coming to our house to collect for the newspaper?" I asked, feeling suddenly brave.

The paperboy slowed down, turned around, and stared into my eyes, measuring whether or not I was worthy of the information. Finally, he said, "You know those brown leather seats filled with straw that the streetcars have that kinda' crunch when you sit down?"

"Yup, I sure do..."

"You know that crunching sound? That's what your body feels like when you've been in bed too long."

I pictured his white face under white sheets. His eyes, shiny and blue, stared out from the bed, looking like they wanted to jump out of his face, out of the bed, down to the lake to fish or go swimming, all by themselves. Two eyes, swimming. He wanted to have fun and instead he was sick. I wanted to reach up and take his hand. I wanted to travel with him in a streetcar right to the end of the line.

"And those great big square windows that you can open up. Have you ever stuck your hand out and tried to grab another streetcar coming the other way?" If I kept talking, he couldn't know how much I wanted to be his friend. We were back in my driveway.

"I catch a streetcar to pick up newspapers every night," he said.

"You mean you have to pay for a streetcar to pick up papers? Do they pay you back?"

"Well, see, we don't have a car…" He fidgeted with his fishing pole. Mother's face peered out the kitchen window. If I went fishing with him, he could keep me safe, and I wouldn't have to listen to my mother's rules or tag along after my sisters.

My house was suddenly too big and my driveway too long. "I'm glad you're not sick anymore. You can cut through any time. If you ever need someone to bait the hook, lemme know. I'm pretty good at it. " The paperboy was already halfway down the driveway when he looked over his shoulder and waved. I noticed for the first time that he walked with a slight limp. I still didn't know his name.

In the fall, Snake, my sisters, our other friend, Spaniel, and I were off to the rink, skates slung over our shoulders, waiting for the yellow streetcar at the corner of Bryant and 44th, listening for the loud, high pitched squeal of streetcar brakes. It cost a quarter to take the streetcar and a quarter to get into the arena. I was thinking about the paperboy, wondering if he had enough money to go skating. I would save my allowance and ask him to come.

Through red bangboards onto the ice, I watched out for skaters going one way. An organist, in a high throne overhead, played Strauss waltzes on a huge, white and gold pipe organ. I pretended I was Tenley Albright skating in heaven. What about the paperboy? Who did he pretend to be? Huck Finn?

Some of the luckier kids had silver bells tied to their skates that jingled as they walked. Would I ever be old enough to have bells on my skates? Would I ever be old enough for change in my pocket? Would I ever get to go fishing with the paperboy or take him skating?

That night, wintry wind whipped elm branches against my windowpanes. Mother and Father were going out, and although Amy, our baby-sitter, was in charge, we'd never see her. Each of us was alone in our rooms. My oldest sister would go out with her teenage friends. My middle sister would watch Dick Clark and Jack Webb and Sid Caesar. I would stay in my bedroom with the door locked, reading *Nancy Drew* and *The Wizard of Oz*.

There were seven doors leading to the outside, seven bathrooms for someone to hide in, seven bedrooms with seven closets. Secrets lurked in dark corners, seven doors to outside wars. Anyone could sneak in. I held my hand over my mouth to keep from screaming. No one could hear me.

Father kept a gun in the very top drawer of his highboy. Before he and Mother left for the night, when Mother was out of the room, I asked Father to take it out and show me how to load it. He cocked his head to one side and examined my face for a moment, then agreed, laying it on the bed, spinning the chambers and demonstrating how to put six gold bullets in separate chambers. Then, he removed them, making me promise never to use it.

Now I had a way to protect myself.

As soon as my parents left, and I knew Amy was sleeping and my sisters were nowhere around, I sneaked into my parents' bedroom, pulled Father's green chair over to the highboy, climbed up on it, and stood on my tiptoes to open the top drawer. I felt around for the barrel and tip. There it was, the gun I could use if I needed it. I ran my fingers up and down the cold steel, feeling my heart thump against my chest, wondering how I would get from my bedroom to the gun, from room to room, counting steps in my mind, imagining myself spinning around faster than whoever was there. Satisfied I could do it, I closed the drawer quietly, raced back to my bedroom, slammed the door shut and bolted it.

I imagined a burly, rough man breaking into my bedroom, busting the brass lock. I pointed the loaded gun at him, aimed, and squeezed the trigger. His blood sprayed all over the wall. His face split open, and dark secrets spilled out. My parents wouldn't like the mess. I woke the next morning, still alive, still afraid.

All winter, I thought about the paperboy and fishing. Father didn't like to fish, and I knew Eric, our neighbor, went ice fishing, so I asked him to take me. Eric and I bundled up in heavy coats and big boots. Eric wore a blue fur-lined cap just like the paperboy's. It was very quiet in his little wood house on the lake. All we heard was the rainy, silvery sound of the slivers of ice against the deep hole he made where he sank his fishing line. I didn't like watching him baiting the hook or pulling in the lines when the fish came up, eyes bulging, gills opening and closing, gasping for air. Frost formed on the ends of my mittens and around my mouth where I was breathing heavily inside my scratchy wool scarf.

I was thinking about the paperboy. Maybe I'd learn to like fishing and we would go fishing together and live in an ice house. I'd even bait the hook. My fingers were very cold and my eyes felt sleepy. Eric carried me home up over snow banks in his big arms. I felt snug in Eric's arms, pretending he was the paperboy. It wasn't Eric's eyes I saw, bleary and slightly moist from too much wind; it was the paperboy's blinding blue eyes, reflecting like a mirror in hot sun. We were together in our golden cocoon, protected from winter and sickness and rules.

I was saving enough allowance to trade with him – he'd take me to his favorite fishing hole and I'd buy him skates with bells. We'd go by yellow streetcar down to the arena, crunching on the brown leather seats. On the way, we'd open up the windows and stick our hands out to touch the tips of elm branches as they flew by, just out of reach.

*Minneapolis resident Carolyn Light Bell has written for **Milkweed Quarterly**, **Minnesota Women's Press** and many other publications. She has organized poetry readings at several high schools and edited literary magazines.*

Young Carolyn and her mother

Joys of Jule-bokking
By Stella Sorbo

Some of my fondest childhood memories are of Jule-bokking in our Norwegian farming area in Freeborn County. It was a Christmas tradition, and Scandinavian Christmases lasted weeks, so we'd practice this wonderful custom over a three-week period that included a week before and a week after Christmas and maybe more, if it wasn't too cold.

Jule-bokking was a tradition of long standing during the 1930s and '40s. The custom consisted of dressing up in costumes made of whatever was handy in Depression era households. Some might even sew something quick and easy on their treadle Singer machine.

The dressing up was nothing fancy, mind you, and could even consist of over-sized clothes belonging to big brothers or a paper facemask or sheets popped over our winter clothes. Dressed in costumes we would travel to our neighbors' houses.

"Come in, Jule-bokkers, come in," our neighbors greeted us. No one ever refused to let us in, though we always thought about that possibility because we were dressed in costumes and behaving noisily, which was an important part of the business of Jule-bokking. We'd sing Christmas songs at the tops of our voices as we approached farm homes.

These were evening events, done under cover of darkness so that people couldn't see us coming, and a real adventure for us Hanson kids who normally stayed put after supper in our gray stucco house on our sixty-acre farm.

One night we went Jule-bokking at the nearest farm, about a quarter mile east of our shiny silver mailbox. The wrinkled grandma smiled and urged us to, "Come in, Jule-bokkers, come in," in her heavy Norwegian accent. Her worn hands held the storm door wide to let us in. There were eight of us in oversized jackets. We wore paper masks, and sheets covered some of our winter clothes. We were eager children with snowy, noisy boots.

"Merry Christmas! Good Jule!" We sang out the words loudly, as good Christmas fools always did.

"Now who can this be?" the grandma questioned as she peered near-sightedly at the little ghost. We giggled self-consciously. It was my little brother, but of course we wouldn't tell, and neither did he.

We made our way through the lefse-smelling kitchen. "Shall we take our boots off?" asked my oldest sister.

"Oh, no, that's all right. Come in!" the grandma replied, her wrinkled face breaking into a smile. We stood in the middle of the living room and sang, "How Glad I am Each Christmas Eve" in Norwegian. She leaned back on the soft, worn sofa, smiled and sighed. We told silly jokes about Christmas trees and such, and as each little act concluded we'd poke the next person to start something new. We ended with our Christmas "pieces" and carols.

We were young enough to hope she did not know who we were, not old enough to know that of course she had already guessed. As we stood in the middle of the clean living room floor, I looked down. Snow was slowly melting from our boots. Her two sons clumped in from milking to take a look at us too. "Now who are you?" they questioned. We were sure they did not know either!

I think the grandma knew we had run out of things to talk about and do because she lifted herself heavily out of her sofa and told us, "Come here, then, Jule-bokkers!" Into the kitchen she led us as our boots left perfect imprints on the worn linoleum floor.

She handed us big, fat peanut butter cookies with real peanuts in them. The sons gave us big red apples. We almost shouted our thanks as we thumped and bumped our way through the storm door. Out through the snow-buried yard, we dashed down the road, full of noise, laughter and cookie eating. We shouted, "Merry Christmas!" and "Good Jule!" again and again.

We turned onto the high road that went right by the grandma's house. Then we saw her through the lighted window. She was down on her knees with a big rag, wiping up our tracks. With her bent back, she had wiped that floor many times, and now she was wiping it again. We had left many puddles.

This kind old Norwegian widow had given us such good, fat cookies and huge apples, and we had gotten her floor all wet. I did not run as fast or shout as much on the way to the next farmhouse.

About ten years later I was home from college at Christmas time. My mother, sisters and I went to visit that neighboring grandma. Her back seemed more bent, but her peanut butter cookies were still offered freely. Her face was more wrinkled than I remembered, but she still had a warm and genuine interest in all of us. As we sat and talked and ate, I looked down at the living room floor, still covered by the same linoleum. Eight children had stood with sixteen wet boots–laughing, singing and joking.

For a minute, that Christmas seemed like a long time ago. With a sudden glow of happiness, I realized that she really hadn't minded wiping up that linoleum floor on that Christmas ten years ago. We had given her a special offering–ourselves, and she had treasured our attention. We had not forgotten her. We loved her. She gave us her love in the shape of fat cookies and big, red apples.

The Hanson Jule-bokkers and their parents in Freeborn, 1939

Important Lessons my Parents Taught Me
By Stella Hanson Sorbo

"All I want for Christmas is that little red-handled broom that I saw in the Freeborn store."

I was about 6 years old at the time, but these were my pre-diary days so the exact date can't be verified. I was thrilled to actually get the broom, and I used it a lot to sweep our hardwood floors. Back then it didn't take much to make us happy.

"My dad has more war bonds than yours does!" we Hanson kids yelled across the railroad tracks, taunting the Gilbertson kids who lived on the next farm. We usually didn't waste much time arguing because they were our closest neighbors of the few playmates we had growing up during Depression days in southern Minnesota. How we knew how many bonds anybody had was a mystery, but we were aware that our dad invested in bonds.

When I was about 8, I got into trouble stealing one of my dad's coins he'd laid out on a table. He kept good track of his money and soon discovered the coin's disappearance. I got caught and had to return the coin. He told me that I couldn't have bought anything with it anyway because it was a coin used in the place where he played cards nearly every Saturday night in Freeborn. I learned that all that glitters is not gold, plus a valuable lesson in morality.

Money was a very tight asset in our childhood days. We girls found work as hired girls as soon as we were confirmed. It was all in the normal, natural process of growing up on a farm at that time. Our brothers hired out before confirmation, and then they worked as hired men on neighboring farms after confirmation.

These experiences gave us all a healthy respect for money and how to earn it because it was usually by the sweat of our brows that we got our pockets filled with coins and bills. But even before we worked for other people we did little jobs around the farm to earn money to purchase notebooks, pencils and candy from Ben Gilmore's grocery store in the little village of Freeborn.

One of our jobs was washing eggs for ten cents a week. Mom probably averaged a flock of about 150 laying hens so there were quite a few eggs to clean. They could be smelly or stained, but gentle rubbing with baking soda or vinegar on a wet rag made from Dad's old underwear could turn most eggs to a beautiful, shiny white.

We had to beware of holding eggs too tightly or scrubbing them too hard or we'd have a squished egg to clean up from the black, hard-packed dirt cellar floor. Worst of all, that egg was wasted, and Mom would have less money to trade for groceries. Cracked eggs could be salvaged for cooking or baking.

We did certain jobs without pay, but we received ten cents a week for milking cows. That was one job I disliked but had to do. Mopping our hardwood floors was a freebie, I think. Dusting, washing dishes and helping prepare meals were regular expectations too, with no pay.

We welcomed chances to earn bigger amounts of money as we grew older, but it did involve more sweat. Helping with grain shocking was hot and itchy. We shelled corn by hand in a sheller for our hens and ducks. We also missed a few days of school when we picked carrots and potatoes from peat fields on crisp fall days. This job paid well, and we earned money for school supplies and clothes.

Baby-sitting for nearby farm families was a good way to earn a dollar or so. Well-behaved kids guaranteed a nice quiet evening. All these jobs made us appreciate the money we earned. I remember being so proud to be able to buy a tan jacket for my grandpa's funeral when I was a young teenager.

I was blessed to be able to work my way through two years of college. Baby-sitting and housekeeping at two different homes got me through college, but it cut into my studying time, which I regretted. During summers I worked in a Bible camp with little chance to spend much money so I saved what I earned. When I started to teach, I owed nothing except a little to my dad, who actually sold one of his war bonds to help me when I was in a really tight spot during my second year of college.

Later in life my mother told me that Dad always saved 10% of what he earned, investing it in the bank or bonds so that they always had something to fall back on. And Mom was able to live frugally off just the interest on those investments in her last years. When they sold the farm, that money bought a little retirement house in Freeborn, where they lived simply and managed well. Mom continued to live there eleven years after Dad died.

These are some important lessons I learned from my folks:

- Don't spend what you haven't got.
- Work for what you earn.
- Share the talents God has given you.
- Save money for a rainy day and for life's end.
- Simplify life by cutting down on wants and needs.

Mom's last year's motto was, "Simplify." I'm trying to put that philosophy into practice. Now that I'm retired from teaching, I've taken away or sold my teaching supplies. This has helped me unclutter closets and rooms. I haven't gotten rid of everything, but every box or sack that left the house was a victory.

I want to want less, buy less, get rid of more, recycle more and give things to people who will use them. As I move into retirement and Social Security, I will get back to my roots and apply those lessons my parents taught me in the 1930s and 1940s, lessons of thrift and common sense.

Haakon and Alma Hanson, 1919

Born and raised in Freeborn, Stella Hanson Sorbo lives in Two Harbors. She is a retired teacher and freelance writer.

Memories of My Country School–District #27
By Lorna Rafness

By happy coincidence my introduction to school involved a party and presents. I was a preschooler, maybe 4 years old, and it was a festive occasion. The school was decorated for Christmas with a tree and all its glittering ornaments. Excitement claimed each child as candy, apples and gifts were distributed. My gift was a cut-and-paste book of fuzzy yellow ducks that I was thrilled to receive. I thought it was the best present a child could get, and I still hold dear the memory of that evening.

My entire family, consisting of myself and my sisters, Shirley and Midge, my older brother Ordell and my parents, Sam and Agnes Severson, attended that Christmas celebration in our one-room country schoolhouse—District #27—in southwestern Minnesota.

That happy event piqued my interest in all things bookish, and in September of 1946, I set off for my first day of school full of exuberant self-confidence. There was no kindergarten so we started as first graders. My sixth birthday had been July 14, and I was eager to enlarge on my personal universe. I got to attend country school for only one year, and soon after the school year began, one of the happiest days of my life occurred. I remember running into the house after school shouting, "I learned to read today!" Nothing else has inspired in me the pure joy I felt at unraveling the mystery of the written word. Who would have thought the words, "Run, Dick, run. Look Jane, see Dick and Spot run!" could arouse such exhilaration. I don't recall attempting to master the three Rs before starting school, and that may be why it was such a memorable event. Could it have happened that way? One minute I couldn't read and the next minute I could? That feeling of elation—the magic of it—stays with me.

It was a good year for me, the most successful of my school years. I can see now that it was because of my attitude and expectations. Life hadn't dealt me any lethal blows yet. At home I was the baby, still sleeping in my crib—literally—but with the sides down. There wasn't any other bed, so whoever was the baby stayed in the crib until the next one came along.

Sometime after I started school, even though a new baby never did come along, I moved into the double bed with my sisters. But I didn't feel like a baby; I felt capable and receptive to the outside world's opening up to me. Although lacking in the competitive sense, I was soon aware that I was the smartest kid in my class—the all-around star–best at lessons, physical activities, and bossing the other kids around. That may not have been a good thing at the age of 6—to peak so early—with nowhere to go but downhill afterward.

However, I confess, there were only four of us in the class, two boys and two girls. Our one-room school was heated with an up-to-date oil-burning floor furnace. One cold winter day the first three grades got to crowd around and stand on the edge of it during our reading class. Little Adeline, the only other first-grade girl, was too timid to interrupt the reading to ask to be excused. She wet her pants standing on the furnace. The sizzling sound and aroma of pee hitting the hot metal alerted everyone in the school to her disgrace. We all just looked at her, but no one laughed. She was so little, and she started to cry. Mrs. Nosbusch told us to go on with our reading and took her aside. I felt sorry for her, but selfishly, more than anything else, I was glad I wasn't Adeline.

The school was just over two miles from our farm, and on nice days we walked home—a long way for a 6-year-old who dawdled and explored along the roadside. More than once I came dangerously close to embarrassing myself before I got to our house. There were no bathrooms at either end, only outhouses. In school the big boys would bang on the outhouse walls when we girls were inside, never failing to scare us. What passed for a playground or schoolyard was weedy, rough prairie with nothing but the two buildings, schoolhouse and outhouse.

There was no structured recreation for District #27 pupils. At recess the girls could jump rope, play catch or games like captain may I. In fall and spring the boys had a makeshift ball diamond with some bats and balls and a glove or two. No wonder they spent most of their time harassing the girls.

My sister Midge remembers playing in the basement of the school when two or three of the bigger boys opened their flies and ran around holding their penises out for the girls to see. Midge was impressed enough to go home and tell our mother about it, who calmly reported it to the teacher. I never heard of any real harm being done on the playground, but I stayed as far away from those menacing older boys as I could.

Mrs. Nosbusch, a tiny attractive young woman just out of normal school, managed to teach all eight grades, up to twenty kids, in that one room. She commanded respect even from the biggest boys who towered over her. A couple of them were almost her age because of starting school late, repeating grades, or taking time off for farm work. Presiding at her desk in the center of the front of the room, she kept everyone under control. The grades were separated and lined up in rows of desks from front to back, starting with the first graders to her right through to the eighth graders on her left. At intervals she would come to each grade or a combination of grades for individualized classes while the others carried on with their studies.

One day little Eddie DeBruckyere, the smartest boy in my class, got bored with doing numbers and whispered to me that he'd crawl back to the bookshelf and get *Cowboy Tommy* for us to read. Eddie was my best friend in school that year, and I think it was because we were the most alike.

Cowboy Tommy was our favorite book. Tommy was a boy our age who lived in the West and took a trip in a stagecoach to visit his great-grandparents in Kansas. He had many adventures such as making friends with an Indian boy named Little Bear, getting to know real cowboys, and acquiring his dog Rover. I loved the illustrations as well as the story. When I look at it now I'm surprised I was so taken with a book tailored to appeal to boys without a single girl in it. My own sexist attitudes hadn't evolved yet.

We were allowed library books only at strictly appointed times so I thought it was quite a wonderful and daring feat for Eddie to take such a risk for both of us. Mrs. Nosbusch was busy with another class, and Eddie didn't think she'd notice him sneak the book off the shelf. Stealthily, getting down on his hands and knees, he crawled back to the bookshelf. Once there he quickly and quietly seized the prized book. Then, illicit goods in hand—thinking himself invisible to her—he started the return crawl to his desk. But just then her voice called out, "I see you Eddie!"

Poor Eddie froze in his tracks. "Now stand up, put the book back, and get to work on your numbers!" It was his turn to be disgraced. Adeline was no longer the only first grader to face public humiliation. This time all the kids laughed. I wasn't laughing though, because he was doing it for me too. I was proud of him. That day he was no longer just my friend, he became my hero and my boyfriend, but I didn't tell him that.

When that school year ended, our family moved into the town of Minneota, and I had to attend second grade there at Public School District #414. On our last day attending District #27, each of us sisters received a parting gift of a book from Mrs. Nosbusch and all her pupils. Shirley's book was *The Chinese Cat,* Midge got *Humpy the Humpback Whale,* and to my astonishment, I was the proud recipient of my very own copy of *Cowboy Tommy.* Little Eddie DeBruckyere himself presented it to me on behalf of the whole school. That softened the blow of our parting of ways. I still have that treasured book, although my own children and others have left their marks on it.

Lorna is in the front row between her sisters Shirley and Midge in this picture of the kids in Country School District #27 in the late 1940s.

Lunch With Grandma
By Lorna Rafness

The winter I was in the third grade, my mother told me that instead of having lunch in school I was going to start eating at Grandma Rafnson's. Grandma lived only two blocks from our school, whereas our house was at least six blocks from it. Still, I was surprised at this new order of things. I liked having lunch in school with the other kids, but I didn't question the plan, I just followed orders. I did wonder though, if it was because we were poor. I was aware of my mother's ongoing struggle to scrape up the cash for lunch money.

Grandma Rafnson, born in Iceland, rented three small rooms from an elderly Belgian couple in Minneota. In her kitchen was a sink and old refrigerator along with a wooden paint-chipped drop-leaf table and three mismatched chairs. In the living room was a dark, shabby couch and one straight-backed chair with an upholstered seat, an oil burner taking up a quarter of the room, and a wooden rocking chair that sat by a little table with a radio. In her bedroom was a fourth kitchen chair, a bed and a dresser with a mirror over it. There was a tiny bathroom with only a toilet in it off her bedroom. Spartan. The exception was her bright-colored knitting yarn, some magazines, a few knickknacks and a deck of cards. Her cards, used to play solitaire or rummy with visiting kids, were so worn-down they were thinned and fragile, and the colors of black and red were dulled and faded. Although she was always chuckling with good will and ever-cheerful, her apartment had a bleakness about it.

On those dark winter days it felt gloomy being at Grandma's, just her and me. But there was plenty to eat, usually boiled potatoes, canned commodity meat and cooked cabbage. She liked sardines and laughed when I refused them. Maybe, living by herself, she had lost all inspiration for baking, but I loved the variety of store-bought cookies she had and graham crackers with milk.

Looking back, I see now that what I thought of as dreariness was the state of poverty she lived in. A poverty clarified by the sunless cold days of winter—with only our two voices filling the bare rooms. Then, the cheap cracked linoleum, the insufficient heat, the sparse furnishings—the totality of meagerness in her life was biting. I didn't understand what felt wrong there, but I knew it wasn't because she was unhappy or discontent. On the contrary, no doubt she felt it was a time of affluence, compared to the earlier Depression years. Then her family truly did suffer from want and hunger. When I was a child, Grandma Rafnson was like a solid rock, never changing, always calm and collected. She seemed to be without emotion except for her very low-key humor. Buddha-like. I would have thought her lack of worldly possessions was natural if I had thought about it at all.

Now I know how little she survived on. It was only the government assistance check; no Social Security, no stocks and bonds, no savings, no other income—except for baby-sitting and the handwork that people bought. It wasn't the depth of poverty where one would go hungry, but without family and community support it could have been. I suspect that my mother paid her what my school lunches cost and that she wanted to guarantee Grandma a daily visitor—at least on school days.

Jona Rafnson of Minneota, age 100

Minneota native Lorna Rafness lives in Mankato, where she and her husband work as writers. The mother of two daughters, she has a master's degree in sociology and is retired from a 32-year postal career.

Sundays With My Folks
By Ted Springer

Sundays were special for our steadfastly middle class, South Minneapolis family in the 1940s. I suppose you could call us functional but boring. We were, however, generally happy, and one reason we remained happy was, I believe, the way we spent our Sundays.

First off, it wasn't a school day. I hated school. No self-respecting 10-year-old boy could like school, could he? Only girls liked school. And second, Mom, Dad, my sister Jeannie Beans (my name for her, which she didn't like, but wasn't that the point?) and I did things together. This meant that we kids got a lot of attention.

Every Sunday morning Mom and Jeanne went to the Congregational Church near Dinkytown. One might say it was a liberal church. Concerned more with reaching out to the disadvantaged, they didn't spend time discussing dogmas like the virgin birth or the resurrection. I remember one Sunday when Senator Hubert Humphrey was invited to give the sermon. Dad said, "He'll talk too long." Sure enough, he did, and our Sunday meal, which Mom put into the oven before church, was burned and barely edible by the time we got home. Being liberal had its price.

Dad attended church too, without fail, every Christmas and Easter, and on rare occasions such as the Humphrey appearance. I was somewhere between, not quite committed. Jeanne eventually got her very own Bible, when she was confirmed, and it had a dazzling white cover and colored pictures. I was envious, but decided that the price in time and dedication to a concept that didn't relate to football was too high. So I never got confirmed, much to the chagrin of Mom and, I suppose, God.

During basketball season, I defected to the Methodist Church in Prospect Park because they had a better team for kids. Today the team would be called "really cool," but then it was "really hot." So much for loyalty. Once basketball season ended, I returned to the Congregational fold, albeit part time.

Sunday afternoons were great because I could look forward to three truly pleasurable activities: going to Elsenpeter's Drugstore, to a movie, and then driving to the airport to watch airplanes take off and land. Elsenpeter's Drugstore, located at Bedford and University, had a soda fountain area furnished with wood-paneled booths, where one could enjoy sinful, delicious treats. Our family would occupy a booth and order various ice cream desserts. My favorite was a sundae made of vanilla ice cream, gooey chocolate sauce, and topped off with a cherry. I don't remember what the others ordered.

Elsenpeter's was the neighborhood fixture, and we stopped there throughout the week for everything from prescriptions to Pepsis, which my gang and I enjoyed two or three times a week. On those occasions, usually after an evening of touch football in the street under the streetlights, we inevitably ordered a Pepsi. I had fallen in love with the high school girl who waited on us at the counter, and that made each visit even more fulfilling. She was, in my mind, beautiful and smart, and to gild the lily, a cheerleader at Marshall High. I thought, "If only I were older."

Pepsi was the only thing we could afford, and we got double the amount that Coke offered in each bottle. Their radio jingle pointed out this fact, and we all knew how to sing the jingle–in fact, I still do. "Pepsi Cola hits the spot. Twelve full ounces, that's a lot. Twice as much for a nickel too, Pepsi Cola is the drink for you."

We were Depression kids, and money was hard to come by. SPAM was a staple on our dinner tables, and Chum Gum (five sticks for a penny) was our choice, even though its flavor lasted about ten chews tops. The kid next door got a bigger allowance so he could get Chum Gum plus two jawbreakers. Geez.

After our Sunday treat at Elsenpeter's, our family headed for the matinee at the Campus Theater on Oak Street. I hoped each week that the movie would be about football, but it almost never was. Most often it was squishy stuff with, ugh, kissing, which was fine with Mom and Jeanne, but Dad (I think) agreed with me in wanting more guy stuff.

Heading home from the Campus, we all looked forward to a casual Sunday supper when we'd eat while listening to *One Man's Family* on radio, a nice but sappy drama about a well-adjusted family.

Minnesota Memories 7

Our third Sunday activity, the one I liked most, was driving to Wold Chamberlain Airport to watch airplanes. There was something awe-inspiring about airplane departures and landings, and we soaked up the romance of it all like blotters. We parked our car adjacent to the landing strip, ready to be entertained by the daring of the pilots, crew, and passengers. We'd sit in the car until we saw an airplane taxiing for takeoff, or one coming in for a landing. Then we'd all pile out of Dad's REO Flying Cloud (America's finest six) and take turns sitting on the ample fenders to watch the breathtaking event.

Ted and Jeanne, sitting on the back of America's finest six

One of the larger planes was the Ford Trimotor, a three-engine metal hulk of a plane. The noise from its engines made our hearts pound, and I tried to imagine what it must be like to watch from a passenger seat as the earth slipped away. I thought that maybe someday I'd be a pilot.

Dad was the only family member to have flown in an airplane. It was a business trip to Duluth, and after he returned we were all agog, asking him questions and reliving the experience as he dramatized the event, knowing he had our rapt attention. One day, on our usual trip to the airport, Dad announced, "Today we are all going for a ride in an airplane." None of us thought he was serious, but he was. So, rather than turning off on the road where we usually watched the action, we headed for the terminal. There was the Ford Trimotor, poised to swallow us up for the ride of our lives, resting on the blacktop, looking romantic, formidable and ominous. We still didn't know whether or not it would happen, but Dad emerged from the ticket office with tickets in hand. Then it hit us. This was for real! Were we scared? You bet!

Our emotions ran the gamut from anticipation and excitement to outright fear. In retrospect, the scene was humorous. All but Dad thought it would be our last day on earth, so before takeoff, we hugged each other and shared goodbye kisses, even though we were all to board the plane together. My heart raced as we taxied to the takeoff area, and I squeezed Mom's hand hard. As we lifted off, our rate of climb was gradual, and I was able to enjoy an almost euphoric feeling of rising through space while watching people and cars below become smaller and smaller.

We must have flown in a giant circle around the Twin Cities, because the whole episode lasted only about fifteen minutes. Surprisingly, that was enough for me. I was actually glad when we lost altitude (gulp) in preparation for landing. We hadn't talked much during the flight because the engines were too loud. After landing, we all hugged and kissed again because, well, we had looked death in the face and survived.

I couldn't wait to tell my friends that I had actually flown in an airplane. I am sure my description didn't capture the sheer drama I'd lived through, but I tried, and in my mind I was more than a little heroic for having had this experience. I showed them the tickets and a picture of the Ford Trimotor. The plane didn't look anywhere as ominous in its picture, but I did my best to embellish my story.

My interest in airplanes continued, and several times I rode my bike to the airport mid-week to watch Navy pilots in training taking off in their Stearman biplanes, touching down briefly, and then heading skyward again. Many landings were rough, with lots of bouncing and uneven descents, and this made watching all the more exciting. They were headed to World War II, and I hoped they survived.

For a few years we continued our Sunday tradition of visiting Elsenpeter's, attending the Campus matinee movies and driving to Wold Chamberlain to watch airplanes. It was still thrilling, and we couldn't help feeling smug because we had "been there and done that." Sundays remained special, and I can't help thinking that those days together helped make our family more tight-knit. After all, the family that flies together stays grounded–er–survives together. Well, you know what I mean.

Minneapolitan Ted Springer worked for B.B.D.O. advertising for thirty years.

World War II Jobs for Women
By Marian Porter Westrum

My husband Lyle and I were married by Reverand Sorenson on June 14, 1941, at the First Lutheran Church parsonage in Albert Lea, and we lived in an apartment on James Avenue and then moved into a little house. We were still newlyweds when Lyle went into the Army in June of 1942. I was clerking at J.C. Penney's in downtown Albert Lea, and I had a very understanding boss. Since he was too old for military service, he said his contribution to the war effort was giving his female employees time off when our husbands came home on furlough or when we had a chance to go visit them.

So it was that I spent several months in Alabama when my husband was stationed at Camp Rucker. When I first got to camp, I applied for a job as secretary to a colonel. I had taken secretarial courses at Albert Lea High School, so I seemed to be just what the colonel was looking for until he mentioned that I would be expected to grant him favors above and beyond the job description.

I said, "No deal," and went to work for a great deal less money at the Post Exchange cigarette counter. Cigarettes sold for ten cents a pack at that time. Selling cigarettes and food during the war may not have been as important as "Rosie the riveter" jobs, but I think the boys appreciated a smiling face and helping hand. On the first night I worked, a soldier approached to engage me in conversation. When I started to speak to him, he turned on his heel and muttered, "Another damn Yankee." The Southerners did not take kindly to my talking to the Negroes (as African-Americans were then called) who also worked at the Post Exchange.

I had a room in a house halfway between the camp and the city of Ozark. The house was on a regular bus run. The day my husband left for maneuvers in Texas, I was on my way back to the room to get ready to return to Minnesota. A soldier who evidently knew my husband was gone told me that he was going to get off the bus and visit me.

When I reached my stop and got up to leave the bus, he got up and started to follow me. "Don't let this man off the bus," I told the driver. "He is not with me." The driver stood up and the soldier sat down.

Later my husband was stationed at Camp San Luis Obispo in California. I again got time off from Penney's to go and stay with him. We rented a room from a friendly older couple for a few months. This time I worked at the Service Club in the cafeteria. I liked the 6 a.m. to 2 p.m. shift for two reasons. I could go see the Pacific Ocean and other sights in the afternoon, and I could get a ride to work with my husband who was picked up at our rooming house at 5 a.m. The car was full so I had to sit on my husband's lap, which was all right with us.

Lyle was shipped to the South Pacific in 1944, and I came back to Albert Lea, where I lived with my parents. I gave birth to my first child in December that year, and Lyle came home and saw his son for the first time when we were celebrating the baby's first birthday.

I worked at J. C. Penney's a couple of summers after that, in the basement checking new stock and pricing merchandise. And of course I shopped there for many years. Everybody did; it was J. C. Penneys!

Marian and Lyle Westrum, June 14, 1941

Albert Lea native Marian Westrum has two children, two grandchildren and a great grandchild. Her son Dex also has a story in this volume.

My First Pair of Skis
By Anastasia "Stacy" Vellas

My brother Connie and I always had a sled. On weekends, Connie and I would put our sister Rose on the sled with us, and we would slide down the big hill north of the house. Other times Connie would hitch our dog Pal to the sled, and Pal would pull the sled around the farm near Swatara, a small town in northern Minnesota.

It was the fall of 1933, and I was 5 years old when Mama sent off to Montgomery Ward for my first pair of skis. It was also the year I started first grade at Swatara School.

One day Daddy said, "Stecy, stand up against this wall and hold your hand up as high as you can reach." He drew a small mark with a pencil at the tip of my finger, got out his tape measure and measured from the floor to the mark.

"What is that for, Daddy?" I asked.

"We gonna buy you a pair of skis. Now that you are going to school, you will need 'em to get to th' main road when snow comes."

Next morning Mama sat down at the kitchen table and wrote out the order to Montgomery Ward in St. Paul. When she finished, she said, "Stacy, I want you to take this letter and put it in the mailbox on the main road. And don't forget to put the flag up so the mailman will stop for the letter." I put on my coat and overshoes and walked down the road to the small barrel Daddy had made into a mailbox. I opened the door on the front and put the letter inside. Then I remembered that Mama had said to put the flag up. I turned it straight up so the mailman could see it, and I ran all the way home.

I was excited when the package arrived containing my brand new skis. They were as tall as my hand could reach. Across the middle of the ski was a leather strap to put my foot through. Daddy helped me put them on and showed me how to tighten the strap over my overshoes. They were a perfect fit. Then he showed me how to push off with the right ski and then follow with the left so I could ski along on top of the snow.

In about the middle of October it began to snow. I could hardly wait for the snow to get deep enough to ski on, and I didn't have long to wait. Soon the road was covered a few inches deep but not enough to need skis because I could still walk on top of the snow. It snowed some more, and soon there was a lot of snow. At first it was slush, and the snow would stick to the bottom of the skis so I couldn't move them. Then the north wind began blowing and dried the slush into a hard crust, and I was able to ski. I was soon soaring over the snow that covered the bog, down to the barn and across the open fields. What a delight my new skis were to me. The day came when I thought I could wear them to school. I thought, "Now I can show everybody my new skis." But, no, no, no, that was not to be.

Daddy said, "Now, Stecy, don' forget when you get to th' road, take th' skis off an' hide 'em in the trees where nom'body see 'em. This evening when you get off bus, wait 'til the bus go; then go get skis an' you come home. We no buy you no more skis."

I was so excited. Over my flour sack cotton slip I put on one of the new print dresses Mama had made. I wrapped my long underwear around my leg at the ankles and pulled my stockings up over them, fastening the top with a garter made from a piece of elastic sewed in a ring. My leather shoes went on and then my overshoes to keep my shoes dry. I put on my new red coat with its lamb's wool collar, and I was ready for school. "I will take good care of my skis, Daddy," I told him.

From then on skis became a part of my life, and for the next three years until my brother started school, I made the three-quarter mile trek to the main road alone. No one ever asked, "Can you go by yourself? Are you afraid?" They just assumed I could do it, so I guess I did too.

Three years later when it came time for my brother Connie to go to school, Daddy decided to make him his first pair of skis. Daddy took two green wood boards and soaked them in water for several days. Then he tied wire around one end of the board and kept tightening the wire until the end of the board was curved at just the right angle. After the wood dried, he removed the wire, brought out his drawing knife and a plane and went to work rounding the edges and bringing the curved end to a point. When the skis were ready, Connie stood on the middle of each ski and

Daddy marked the place for the strap. Then he cut out a slit through the board and put a strap through each ski. Now we each had a pair of skis.

Our log house was perched halfway up the treeless hill. My Grandfather had cleared about thirty acres of land after he homesteaded the place in 1901. We could ski off in any direction for over a quarter of a mile and still see the house. The poplar and birch trees that grew outside the cleared area were bare in the winter and we could see far and wide. We never got lost.

On weekends after Third Guide Lake had frozen over we would ski across the lake to the O'Brien's place and play with the kids. The lake had two or three feet of ice, and a couple feet of snow lay on top which was whipped flat and hard by the wind. It was wide open, and the flat surface made it easy to ski fast. Today they call it cross-country skiing. It was the only kind of skiing we knew back then, a joy and a necessity when you lived in the woods near Swatara. Skiing was a fundamental part of my early life.

Swatara, where Stacy went to school

Stacy Vellas moved from Swatara to California in 1944. After working as a waitress and a field worker, she became a teacher in 1973. The mother of five sons, she lives in Brawley, California.

The Alleys Were Magical
By Julie Zappa

Growing up on St. Paul's east side in the early 1960s left me with wonder-filled childhood memories of summertime freedom. We escaped the house, school and parents on our Sting Ray bicycles, able to wander and explore carefree. The alleys became avenues to adventure. Add to that my first schoolgirl crush, and you have a recipe for romance. I never got the boy, but I believe those two-wheeled adventures left me the motorcycle enthusiast I am today.

Matty flies by on his bike. I yell, "Going to Devil's Hill?" He stops the Sting Ray with a skid, looks back to measure the black line left on the sidewalk.

"Yeah, wanna buck?"

I jump off the front porch rail, ankles buzzing when they hit the ground, and run down the hill toward Matty. Here on the slope, I can stand and reach my leg over the banana seat. His bike has the coolest seat, night-sky-blue with glitter glints. Matty leans his bike toward the hill. I slip in place between his warm-moist back and the sissy bar.

He takes off fast, doesn't even say "hold on." I grab his belt loops as he rises from the seat to pedal, pushing for speed. The breeze sends the scent of him past my face. I hear the Joker clicking over the spokes. Matty attached the playing card to the front fork of his bike with a clothespin. It reminds me to keep my toes clear of the tires. I decide to clip a Queen of Hearts on my bike, and picture it fluttering in the danger zone.

Devil's Hill: a straight up and down alley between the Arcade Theater and Winkler's TV. The alley shoots right out into Arcade Street traffic. We come to the top from the back way, a more gradual incline so we don't need to get off and walk. Matty circles the bike at the top, watching cars down below.

"Ready?" he yells. "Go!" I scream.

He tenses forward, still standing, pumping the pedals, back moving furiously from side to side. I raise my face to the sky, eyes shut, feeling the wind and breathing in Matty. On the way back home, we pass a house with a huge, wondrous plum tree trapped in the backyard behind a white picket fence, a plum tree regularly ravaged by the fastest and bravest of the neighborhood boys. Matty has me slip off the bike and begin walking home. I make it back to the porch and see him pedaling up the sidewalk, one hand on the V shaped handlebars and the other holding his shirt bottom, turned up to make a basket that gently cradles all those fat, ripe plums. He gives me the biggest one.

"Matty got a dirt bike," announces Daddy. "Stay away from him when he's on that thing." The engine whines up and down the alley. It's close to dusk. I run outside. The air smells woodsy, the sharp-smoke smell of trash burning night, a city child's campfire. Heavy metal trash drums, turned umber-orange with use and age, line the alley like hibernating bears all week, waiting for tonight. Tonight their sides, cracked open by rust, let fire light shine through.

It's getting dark. Mothers call in the younger kids. Golden light and radio waves flow from kitchen windows. Babies cry. Young couples argue. I remember last fall, when Matty squirted lighter fluid into a flaming barrel. Fire shot up as tall as the apple tree. Heat pushed out from the flame created a warp that ate up time and space. Then the flame died down to a controlled crackle. Oily ash filled the air, and Matty was screaming, covering his face with the crook of his arm.

Next morning, I sat with Matty at his kitchen table, watching him eat Lucky Charms. His hair was cut in a buzz cut, necessary to get rid of the singe, his eyelashes short, stiff stubs. His mother said, "Told you God was gonna get you for all that preening and fussing with yourself. Stare in a mirror too long and you'll see the devil looking back at you. I hope you've learned your lesson."

Matty let loose a laugh and shoved another spoon of Lucky Charms into his mouth. Before long, his curls grew back, and his dark lashes came in even thicker. The accident didn't stop him from staring in mirrors, riding his Sting Ray or loving the alleys.

Minnesota Memories 7

I love the alley too, and on this July night, it becomes a shower of falling stars. Twisting-twirling blackened paper tendrils spiral up from the drums, break loose, and flicker like fireflies or confetti falling up. A hot ticker tape parade of gold-glitter-red. White flecks of ash fly through the summer air like snow. Farther down the alley, a bottle pops from the heat.

Matty screams by. I stand and wait. On the way back, he downshifts, pulls to the side. He flicks his head to a space behind him, a sign for me to squeeze on. I wrap my arms around his waist, and we fly down a fiery gauntlet.

Julie Zappa and her 1968 Huffy

Julie Zappa lives on St. Paul's east side. She has had poetry and essays published in **Artworld Quarterly, Minnesota Poetry Calendar, Sidewalks** *and other literary journals.*

When Bigfoot Lurked in Austin
By John D. Tripp

I am sitting in a dark movie theater. Even though my eyes are glued to the screen and my whole body is tense, I can feel Brian sitting to my right. I am tense because I know, I just know, that Bigfoot is going to get the couple relaxing in their house onscreen. They can smell something odd and are hearing noises coming from outside. I am trying to telepathically warn them not to look out the window or open the door and go outside. But they are not listening to me. They're doomed. I just know it.

Brian does not seem as engrossed as I am. He is 12, two years older than I am. That makes him a "big kid." I worship Brian. He lives in Austin, the same town as my grandparents, while I live 185 miles away in Duluth. I only get to see him when we come to visit Grandma and Grandpa. He always acts happy to see me and never treats me like a little kid. He is fun and outgoing and has a huge smile with huge front teeth, bordering on buckteeth. He has lots of friends and I think he is cool. When I play with him, I feel cool too.

He asked me to go to the movies with him tonight. I was so excited. Dad let me go and that made me even more excited. We (meaning Dad) are on vacation and much more relaxed, so I get to be a little spoiled. The movie is about Bigfoot and my excitement grew. It's a wonder my head didn't explode from sheer joy.

As we waited outside the theater, Brian turned to me. "Now don't get scared. Bigfoot isn't real; it's just a movie. Don't be a baby." He tried to scold me to look cool in front of his two friends who joined us. It didn't bother me because I could hear in his voice he didn't mean it. He was just trying to tease me. But saying Bigfoot isn't real? Ha! Even big kids don't know everything. Oh, Bigfoot is real all right. I just know it.

The first part of the movie is about the Loch Ness Monster and the Abominable Snowman. Though I am watching, I don't pay any attention. That part just passes right by me. I am entranced with Bigfoot because he is here. He lives here, in the U.S. I have read all the Bigfoot books my neighborhood library has, and there are a lot (I have a high reading level for a 10-year-old). He could be right here in Minnesota.

The man on screen has gotten out of his chair to investigate the strange noises. Despite my warning to him, he opens the door. And there is Bigfoot, filling the doorway, looking back at the man. The man and his wife scream and girls in the audience scream and I scream too. Bigfoot is in that guy's house!

I feel my hand start to reach toward Brian's. I want him to protect me. He's a big kid; he won't let Bigfoot get me. I hear people in the audience laugh at the people who scream, and I hear Brian laugh too. He turns to me and snickers, "I told you not to be scared."

My fright-adrenalin-rush has worn off, and my hand returns to my lap. "I wasn't scared," I tell him defiantly. "All the people who screamed startled me." Brian turns back toward the screen with a small smile on his lips. I don't think he believes me. I don't think I believe myself either.

We are standing outside waiting for my dad to take us home. Brian's friends have left with their own rides. It is a warm summer evening, and the air is very still. Brian scolds me again for getting scared, but again I can tell he doesn't mean it. I think he finds it funny that I was scared. I know he will laugh, but he will be careful not to make me feel bad for being scared. Not because I am a little kid, but because he is cool.

Dad brings us home, and I say goodnight to Brian as he walks toward his house. It is still warm and now it is very quiet. Grandma and Grandpa live close to the commercial area where the movie theater is, but it is still on the edge of town. The big woody area behind their house muffles the noises from downtown and the other theater nearby, a drive-in, from penetrating this far.

I say goodnight to my parents, after telling Mom all about the great movie. I have figured out by now that it was just a very tall man in an orangutan suit, but the image has stayed with me. I say goodnight to Grandma and Grandpa. They are very old, and I have never really felt close to them. Not like my other grandma and grandpa.

My younger sister is already in bed asleep. I go into the bathroom and change into my pajamas. I run the water in the sink so Mom will think I am brushing my teeth (I hate brushing my teeth). I go pee, flush, and climb the stairs to the second floor to Uncle Jackie's bedroom. He is in his bed, sleeping, and I crawl into my bed on the other side of the room. Mom comes up to tuck me in and open the window. It is very warm up here on the second floor; maybe a breeze will cool it off.

I think about the movie, and now that I am safe in bed and alone, I laugh at myself for being scared. It was a very bad-looking orangutan suit, but wow that first glimpse when you don't know what it is. I am glad I was able to spend time with Brian. I wonder what we will do tomorrow. Maybe we'll go to the swimming pool on the newer side of town and...

I wake with a start. I am wide awake, and my blood is pumping, my heart is beating so fast. Something woke me. What? I look across the room, and Uncle Jackie is still asleep in his bed. What was that?

I hear something outside. The window is still open and I can hear it outside. Oh no! I know what it is. Bigfoot. I just know it. He's here. Outside the house. "Please..." I whisper. "Oh please no..."

I want to get out of bed and look out the window. But I know if I do that, he will be there, looking back at me. He'll see me and know where I am.

It doesn't matter that I am on the second floor, twenty feet off the ground. He is looking in the window at me right now. I pull the sheet over my head. Mom has folded the blanket down at the bottom of the bed because it is too hot to sleep with it. I reach down, not looking, and in a lightning move pull the blanket up over my head. I have to do it fast or else Bigfoot will see me and maybe try to reach in through the window or even try to growl at me.

I am under the sheet and blanket. I am so hot the sweat is pouring off me, and it's hard to breathe. But I can't move and won't move because Bigfoot is right outside the window, and he will see me. Mom and Dad will find me suffocated in the morning, and they won't know what happened because Bigfoot will be long gone by then, laughing because he got me.

I try to whisper loudly for Uncle Jackie, but he sleeps on, and I try to whisper-yell for Mom, but she is on the first floor and won't hear me, and Bigfoot is looking at me through the window and he will get me and I don't know how he can look through a second floor window, but it doesn't matter because he right there – right here!

At some point I fall asleep and wake up to the sun. Only the sheet covers me so some self-preservation must have kicked in. I laugh at myself for being so scared last night. It was the movie that got me believing Bigfoot was here. Of course he wasn't here; he was too busy terrorizing campers up in the Pacific Northwest. Still, I don't think I will tell Brian. As cool as he is, this is make-fun-of worthy material. And besides, how could Bigfoot look in through a second story window? Did he have stilts?

I get up and go downstairs to see if we will have pancakes for breakfast. I like the way Grandpa cuts up my pancakes. But as I go down the stairs, I hurry past the window at the landing and make sure not to look out. Because if I do, I will know. I do know. Bigfoot was here. I just know it.

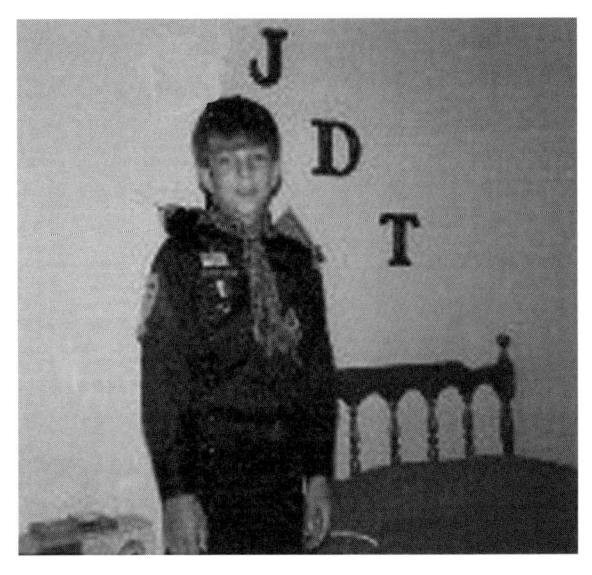

Young John D. Tripp

Twin Cities resident John D. Tripp was born and raised in Duluth . Except for a year in California, he has lived in Minnesota all his life.

Farm Chores
By Kathy Moe

Every farm and a number of city dwellings had chicken barns in the 1930s and 1940s. Poultry provided the family with meat and eggs. Chicken chores were a reality for most farm kids, especially girls and younger children.

Chickens could be ordered straight run or sexed. The straight run would have about an equal number of roosters and hens. Someone at the hatchery checked the sexed group, and this order usually only contained a few roosters per hundred poults. Roosters were preferred for meat because they grew a little larger than hens.

People ordered chicks early in the spring and put them in the brooder house under a lantern or heat lamp. A brooder was a square metal hood that was heated to keep the chicks warm. After electricity arrived, it was much safer to heat with a light bulb than it had been when the heaters were kerosene or oil fired.

The little chicks needed a lot of attention and supervision. As they grew they were allowed more room to run, and as spring warmed up the air, they were allowed outside the brooder house to run in a fenced yard. The fence prevented them from being picked off by some predator. When they reached a larger size, they might be allowed to roam freely. They were a great asset to a yard or a potato patch as they ate a lot of bugs.

As fall grew near, preparations were made to move the pullets into the chicken barn to take the place of the older laying hens, which were either sold or canned for winter eating. The chicken barn would be cleaned out carefully and aired out to cut down on diseases.

The biggest problem of the fall roundup was catching the pullets that had been used to running freely. They often went back into the brooder house in the evening, and if someone remembered to close the door behind them, these were easier to catch. Chicken wranglers usually worked in the dark with a flashlight so the chickens couldn't see them. We used a long pole with a hook on the end to catch the chicken by the leg, and then someone carried it to the chicken barn.

There were always a number of chickens that roosted in the trees, and these were always a little harder to catch. It took several nights to move most of them, and then finding the few on the loose might take a few weeks longer. A catcher had to be at the right place at the right time to get them.

Chicken chores were considered the easiest ones on the farm and often given to the younger children. It was not difficult to fill the water containers and place ground feed in the long troughs that were close to the ground so the chickens could reach. Picking the eggs was a little more difficult as the picker had to reach into the nests for the eggs. There were always a few hens that wanted to sit on the nest and hatch their eggs, and they did not give them up easily. A few of them were very good at pecking at any hand that reached in.

As we kids grew older, our parents gave us more responsibility. One chore consisted of a hike to the pasture to bring the cows home for milking. Most were willing to be relieved of their load of milk and walked home on their own at milking time, but a few would always procrastinate at the far end of the pasture. When Uncle Joe moved to town, we adopted his dog. Shep was a very good herder, and all he needed was for someone to point at the pasture and whistle, and he would bring the cows home.

Richard, James, Donna, George and Kathryn, 1945

We often watched in the barn as the cows were milked. Dad usually kept about fifteen milking cows. This was enough to produce our own milk and cream with a little cream to be sold to the Morgan Cooperative Creamery.

Mother helped with the milking chores and used the separator to separate the milk from the cream. After she took the household supply, she put the cream for the creamery into a can that was stored down in the cool of the well pit until it was picked up by the truck. The remaining milk was mixed in a large barrel with ground feed, mineral supplement and water to feed the pigs.

Pigs are very greedy eaters, and they could make a lot of noise while they waited impatiently for their food to be poured. The milk cows, feeder cattle and horses on the farm were fussier eaters. They liked their dry food and water fed to them separately. There were several large water tanks of cool water for the larger animals. The milk cows also had small waterers beside their stanchions.

Dad worked hard when he first bought the farm and built a large water tank in the haymow of the barn. From there the animals were watered through a gravity flow system. He was very proud of his accomplishment. Once a day he ran the pump to fill the overhead tank with water. We were supposed to watch the overflow pipe to tell when the tank was about full, because then we should shut off the system. If water started running across the dooryard, we knew we didn't catch it in time.

The chores for the larger animals were considered a little more dangerous, and the older boys did those chores. Silage would have to be thrown down from the silo. Ground feed from the bin was placed on top of each individual cow's feed pile. Bedding straw was pushed down from the haymow and spread for the cows. It kept them more comfortable and clean for milking.

While the cows were fed in the barn, the feeder cattle were fed outside in long wooden feeders. They were arranged so that someone could walk out the door of the feed room attached to the barn and step straight into the feed bunk. Walking along the bunks to the far end of the system kept the person high and dry in muddy weather and also out of the way of large animals that were jostling for position along the bunks.

As I grew older, I was asked to help with the feeding chores during spring planting or fall harvest. My mother was a little leery of that idea as I was an animal lover, and she thought I did not have the proper respect for these huge creatures. She would watch me walking the bunks and scold every time I stopped to pet one of the large animals on the head.

Her fear may have come from the fact that she helped with the milking much of the time. The large cows had no qualms about stepping sideways and knocking someone off the milk stool or putting a foot in the milk pail, or worse yet, kicking someone who was walking behind them. Our milk cows disappeared in the early 1950s, when Mother had been kicked one too many times and economics made it easier to buy pasteurized milk in town.

Mechanization and the ability to buy things in town marked the beginning of the decline of the kinds of farms we had when I was growing up. With labor saving devices, fewer farms and less diversity on those remaining farms, few kids today are expected to pitch in and perform the kinds of chores that were a natural part of my childhood.

My sister Donna, 1930

Springfield resident Kathy Moe has been collecting family history for years in order to write stories and chronicle events to hand down to children, grandchildren, nieces and nephews.

Mother's Legacy
By Kathy Moe

Someone said, "History is small stories happening to small people." Everyone has a story. If only they would take the time to tell it.

A number of years ago, the people in Springfield compiled *The City of Springfield*, a book about the city founders and city beginnings. Just recently they completed another book, *The People of Springfield*. Area residents were asked to contribute their family's story. So many interesting ideas were received that all couldn't be published in the book. Some families had indeed saved not just family genealogy but also stories about the pioneering days. It reminded me of the treasure trove that Mother left us.

While cleaning out the house after the death of my parents, we found a box containing diaries and ledgers Mother had kept. There were differences of opinion about whether they should be kept as history or discarded as personal. History won out, and they sat in the box in my house for a number of years.

The information contained in them is fascinating. A person can read and follow the family's trials, growth and prosperity. The record of family life is fantastic. Mother managed to keep a written record for over fifty years and not have a bad thing to say about anyone.

Both my parents came from large families, and the extended family kept in touch. Mother and her siblings continued the tradition with a lifetime of visits and letters with one another that kept them in the know about each other's activities and general news of the neighborhood. It was always interesting to see Mother and her sisters get together for a good gabfest, where we cousins were left to entertain ourselves with occasional supervision by one of the ladies who saw when we were up to mischief.

Education was considered an advantage in this family. The country school was a mile away from their home, and regular attendance was encouraged through grade school. Country roads and transportation were a problem so Mother was sent to board with relatives so she would have the advantages of a high school education. On weekends she was taken to Clements and put on the train for the trip to her grandparents who lived sixteen miles away in Springfield. To get there, she had to change trains in Sleepy Eye.

She spent the week and returned home on weekends when weather permitted. We did not understand Mother's affection for several girl cousins until we realized they grew up almost as sisters while Mother was separated from her own family.

Grandpa was no doubt very proud of a daughter who made it to teachers college and prepared for an occupation in one of the area country schools. This was nipped in the bud when she was brought home to help care for her terminally ill mother
.

Cancer was not mentioned in polite society at the time, and when Mother told us later of what had taken her mother, she stated the fact almost as if cancer were a dirty word we should not hear. It was no doubt a painful memory for her, thinking of a mother who suffered through the disease at home when not much was known about it and little could be done to help or make her comfortable.

Dad was the boy around the corner, actually a farm a few miles away, the second oldest of four boys. He also believed in education. Although he did not attend high school, he spent a year at a business college and another at Dunwoody Institute learning welding and mechanical fabrication. His love for figures and tinkering kept him entertained all his life and helped make his farm a prosperous operation.

His father owned land but could not start all his boys in farming. The two oldest worked out for other farmers. In the summer they went with threshing crews that worked their way through North and South Dakota. In the 1920s they were paid fifty cents or a dollar a day plus breakfast, dinner and supper plus several good lunches in between.

They slept in their car or the farmer's barn. Fresh straw stacks could be comfortable places to rest. With one change of clothes to their name they considered themselves lucky if the farm wife would wash their spare set of clothes at the end of the week's work. Working this way, the two brothers were able to put down payments on farms a quarter mile from each other. They worked together and shared machinery all their lives to make farming more economical.

Mother married Dad in June of 1929. The church wedding was followed by a reception at the home of the bride's father. Pictures show the relatives gathered on the lawn on a fine afternoon. The pictures also show a car with chains on. When questioned about the chains, Dad said that it had rained the day before, and he wasn't sure that they would be able to make it through the area's muddy roads.

After a honeymoon in the Black Hills, they lived together 57 years. They started farm life and raised a family through the Depression and World War II, when money was tight and rationing put limits on what they could buy when they could afford it.

Mother's diaries started in 1942. No doubt one of her children had given her the five-year diary as a birthday present. Inside the front cover, the penciled price shows 25 cents. It's hard to imagine when she found time to make the daily entries, yet they continued faithfully for most of her life. The ledgers started with their married life as Mother kept track of all household expenses. Many of her ledger entries centered around the groceries and meals that kept the family well fed on a limited budget. The clothing purchased was mentioned by kind and size. There were also often notations as to whether the clothing wore well and was really a good purchase. Christmas and birthday gifts for the family and friends were also tabulated carefully. The records she kept provide a valuable record of the era.

Education was considered very important to the family. Both Mother and Dad had continued their educations, Mother with teachers college and Dad with technical college. Both had an appreciation for books. Three of the five of us went on to further education after high school.

We were in the country where certain sections of the township were assigned to a school district. Because the Clements school was closer to us than the district we were living in, we were allowed to go to school in Clements.

The school was one mile from our home. In nice weather in spring and fall, we often walked, especially if there was fieldwork to occupy the family. On other occasions Mother would come to get us. This provided a good reason to visit with two of her sisters who lived in town.

The Clements school was a large, square wood building. It had an upstairs that was used at one time, but by the 1940s the upstairs was considered unsafe for crowds and was used just as storage. We had two classrooms with four grades in each. The class sizes varied. By the time I was in the upper classroom in the late '40s, consolidation had started in Minnesota school districts, and our class size about doubled.

Beside each room was a long, narrow room for coats, boots and lunch bags. There was another large room about the same size as our classrooms. We were considered a progressive district in the late 1940s and early '50s, and this room was used to serve us hot lunches. Two of the local ladies were our cooks, and both knew all the children and their families. Our lunches were tasty as well as nutritious. Another sign of progress were the indoor restrooms in the basement. The outhouses still stood on the school property where they were last used.

The nice thing about belonging in one district and going to school in the other was that we went to two Christmas programs and two end of the year picnics. One program we had to perform in while the other we could relax and watch. The picnics were always a lot of good potluck food for lunch and many games and contests. Attending provided a good opportunity to visit with all the neighbors.

Clements was in the center of a circle of four cities with high schools. When time came to start ninth grade, the students were going in four different directions. We lived south of town so we headed to the high school in Springfield. The owner of our school bus lived in Clements and started his route there. We could watch out of the window at home and see him coming down Main Street. By the time he reached the cemetery a half mile away, we had better be headed out the door because our grove obstructed our view of him after he passed the cemetery. If we missed seeing him leave town, he often surprised us at the end of our driveway.

The ride to high school was about an hour. The morning and evening rides were a good time to do homework. A number of us would sit together to work on it, and that made it much more fun. Mother and Dad often wondered why I carried a pile of books home each day but seldom looked at them once I arrived.

Music was considered a part of our education. Donna joined Uncle Ted's daughters and two neighbor girls for the ride to Redwood Falls, where they took piano lessons. Mother kept careful track in her ledgers and diaries of the cost of these lessons and also whose turn it was to take the girls for the 25-mile trip to Redwood.

Clements also had a community band for years, and my older brothers both learned to play the clarinet while still in grade school. Donna had a saxophone that she continued to play all through high school. The boys did not play in the high school band because we lived 20 miles from Springfield and rode the school bus. The band met before school started so it did not fit in the schedule.

Piano lessons were also in my schedule. There was a piano teacher in Clements who gave lessons in her home, and I could walk there after school. If Mother was not waiting outside her house when I finished, I knew to walk the block and a half to Aunt Hattie's. The enjoyment of reading and music was perhaps the greatest legacy we received. All of us have continued to read and learn throughout our lives.

Reading Mother's journals helped bring many of these memories into focus. I'm glad she took the time to write them and that I found the time to read them.

Kathy with her family

Growing Up in the Depression and War Years
By Ken Jenkins

In my formative years, we did not live anywhere very long. Times were tough in the 1930s. My dad was a barber so he had work, but he had to move around a lot. When I was very small we lived in the village of Itasca, northwest of Albert Lea, in a small house behind Itasca School. The village no longer exists, nor does the school, but the Itasca grotto or rock garden still attracts tourists and provides a beautiful backdrop for photographs.

I must have been like Dennis the Menace because I was always running off and getting into things. At the bottom of the hill was a junkyard for old boxcars, and this area became a hobo jungle. My mother found me there one day when I was about 2 years old, listening to hobos tell their stories. Another time she found me in the grotto, a neat but dangerous place for a little kid to play. And still another time she told me I couldn't go out to play because people had seen a feral boar in the neighborhood, a dangerous animal. Do you think that stopped me? No way! I went looking for the boar when nobody was paying attention to me.

Our next home was in Matawan. The only event I remember there was being taken on a motorcycle ride that scared me stiff. I have not been on a motorcycle since. We moved to Kiester, and then to Manchester, where we stayed for three years. I started school in Manchester in 1935, but cold weather that got down to 30 below zero that year kept little kids home for a week.

There was a man from McAllen, Texas who came up during summers with a portable movie projector and showed free movies at parks and public places in small towns on Saturday nights. Some of them were even talkies. Of course, it didn't get dark enough to see the movies until 9 or later, so this kept the town awake until a late hour. There was a grouchy old man who lived over the store next to the lot where they showed the films, and he objected to the noise we made while watching the movie. One time he heated up a bunch of Indian head pennies in a frying pan and threw them down so we kids would pick them up and burn our fingers. I still have a number of those pennies.

Manchester had a one-room school. I was naturally left handed, but the common belief then was that lefties needed to be cured. Every time I picked up a pencil, the ruler came down on my hand until I learned to use my right hand.

Students at Manchester School. Ken is on the left, and his sister stands behind him. Billy Christensen's dog even got into the act.

We moved to the big town of Albert Lea, and I had to walk past the American Gas Company to get to school. They had a big strike that year with lots of violence, and although I was supposed to walk around that area, I walked right through it and managed to survive. Another misadventure was the time I found some .22 caliber bullets in someone's garage and decided to make noise by hitting them with a hammer. That sure did the trick, but after my mother rushed out and found me, I had a hard time sitting down for a while.

Our next move was to an apartment over a store on North Broadway, and I went to the brand new Lincoln School. Dad had acquired the barbershop in the Hyde Building downtown, where he stayed until his retirement. While living downtown, I became what you might call a street urchin, and I sold newspapers and magazines in every beer joint in town. One of my best customers was Gus Westrum, the policeman. Gus always had a nickel for *Liberty* magazine if I could find him off duty at the station near our apartment on Broadway. Gus and I have a permanent connection because I married his youngest daughter Maxine.

Leo, Harold and Maurice Duffy, Mark Jones and Dick Nelson, whose dad owned the Rex Café, became my downtown friends. When Fountain Lake ice broke up every spring, we would get aboard the ice blocks and push them around to see if we could knock each other off. In summer it was always fishing and swimming. Whenever I wander back to Albert Lea, I still get together with Mark Jones for lunch.

I retired as a newsboy and went to work setting pins at the Town Club Bowling Alley. I also shined shoes at Dad's barbershop. People took good care of their shoes and kept them for a long time, and they didn't mind paying a kid to shine and buff them while they talked with the barber and other customers about politics, fishing, sports and everything else. I was a young teenager then, and our family had moved to a house.

At age of 14, several big changes occurred. I discovered girls and I started roller-skating at the rink downtown in the evenings and on weekends. I also got a job at Moulton's Super Market delivering groceries. I did not have a driver's license, but they said I should tell the folks at the courthouse that I was 16. So I did. I paid my 35 cents and got a valid license, but I still didn't know how to drive. Luckily Moulton's needed a man in the meat market so that is where I went and stayed until the war ended and the men came home and got their jobs back. At that point, I became unemployed.

After graduating from Albert Lea High School in 1947, I went to work driving for Yellow Cab. This is where I met Maxine, who was a dispatcher. Drivers were not allowed to fraternize with the dispatcher because she was only 14 or 15 years old at the time, so it was quite a while before we got together.

I joined the Navy in 1948, and that was my life for the next twenty years. Kids growing up during the Depression and World War II had a far different experience than kids growing up now. We were given independence at an early age, but we were also expected to work. I think those experiences were very positive. You learned to take care of yourself, and you also learned the value of a nickel. These early lessons provided a strong foundation for life.

Ken Jenkins lives in Las Vegas. He has a master's degree in history.

The Frosty Trap
By Louise M. Aamodt

I was terrified of missing the school bus. Mother, unable to leave her daycare center located in our basement and drive me to school, had long ago struck the fear of God into me about how she would react if I missed the bus. To this day, my stomach lurches when I hear the unmistakable whining, grinding engine of an approaching school bus.

Many farmers in those days built sheds at the end of their long driveways to shelter their children from the frigid winter winds while waiting for the bus. My yellow shed had a north-facing window so I could see the broad bus lights as they wound their way down the long hill before passing our house. The trick was to stay inside the relative warmth of the shed as long as possible, then dash the last fifty yards to the end of the driveway in time for the driver to see me and stop. My parents had given up on placing the shed closer to the road where vandals had frequently tipped it over.

On winter mornings, I often entertained myself by pulling off one mitten and scratching designs with my fingernails on the ice coating the shed's windowpane. First I scraped the necessary viewing hole to watch for the approaching bus. Then I wrote messages, drew hearts around the initials of my latest crush or used the side of my fist and my fingertips to melt little footprints, making it look as if a barefoot baby had marched across the window.

One frozen morning, I was delighted to find that the frost had etched beautiful, delicate patterns across the entire windowpane. I automatically scraped open a viewing hole, and then I admired the frosty art. The designs were too lovely to destroy, too intricate for my clumsy hands to touch. No, this natural work of art required a more personal response–warm and tender. The window *begged* me to lick it.

Every Northern child has been admonished not to stick his or her tongue onto anything cold outside, and I was no exception. But the hardest thing to ignore, after all, is something you've been warned not to do. As if in a trance, I touched the very tip of my tongue to the frosted, leafy pattern. And there, of course, it stuck.

At first it felt like licking a Popsicle from the freezer, but it didn't melt and release like the frozen treats always did. In fact, the longer I tried to wiggle my tongue around to free myself, the more of it stuck to the windowpane. How could something so lovely be so treacherous?

Even in my predicament, I swiveled my head to peek through my little viewing hole. Far away, up on the hill, I saw the school bus, and my heart thumped wildly to the rhythm of the blinking lights as it made a distant stop. The lights swung my way then, picking up speed as the bus descended the hill. It was almost time to make my customary dash to the end of the driveway, and my tongue was not one bit closer to freedom. I heard the engine whine as the bus slowed. My god, it was actually close enough to hear, and I was still trapped in the shed. I didn't even consider the possibility of staying there until help arrived. Oh no, missing the bus was not an option. My mother had seen to that.

I could no longer see the bus through the trees near the driveway so I knew it was very close–close enough to creep to a halt any second. I knew what I had to do, and it was now or never. I closed my eyes, wrenched my head back and ran. I raced with tears stinging my eyes and the metallic taste of blood filling my mouth. I ran as if the Hounds of Hell were nipping my heels, propelling me forward to the gaping bus doors.

And I made it. I had sacrificed a little piece of my self, but I made it. Despite the pain, I would not have to endure some unknown, but surely horrific punishment for missing the school bus.

The next morning I sadly contemplated the little scrap of skin frozen on the windowpane. It looked alien there, plastered to the glass. With a little stick, I scraped off and thus destroyed all evidence of my poor judgment. I never told my parents what happened that morning because I just knew they would say, "I told you not to lick anything cold outside!" One way or another, all of us Minnesota kids learned that lesson.

Louise Aamodt is a Lakeville teacher, mother and writer who focuses on animal rights issues.

Hooked
By Kimberly Mark

Friday: It is early afternoon, and I sit in my office mechanically nibbling pretzels. My phone's message light is on, and papers are scattered all over my desk. The cursor on my computer screen blinks in an unfinished e-mail. I stare at my beige cubicle wall and think only of the north lake, with its leaning birch border and whispering wind that protects it all. I shake off the vision long enough to dial Kevin at work, hoping he is ready to leave.

We are finally out of the city limits, the most sluggish part of the three-hour trip. It is early, and the weekend traffic has not clogged Garrison yet. Kevin flies the Chevy as I watch the pulse of Lake Mille Lacs. Trees flash springtime browns and greens and their shadows mix in the sunlight. We break into a clearing and see anglers on the lake. Their tiny boats create a quiet village of their own.

First the line goes through the eye, then through the loop. Twist it around and around and through the loop again. Pull tight and cap the hook with a red plastic skirt. Snap the bobber on and cast into the glass surface. The entire setup takes me about five minutes, but years ago, when I first learned, it would take me at least three tries before the hook was truly attached to the line. Kevin has shown wonderful patience with me, and I have slowly become one of the guys. I wait a moment, and the bobber slowly sinks out of sight. I set the hook and start to reel. A silver flash appears at the surface. A twitch brings water splashing and sparkling in the sinking sunlight. It is my first crappie of the season.

Evening. I am in bed and restless. Although there is no place I would rather be, I still have a hard time sleeping in the rustic cabin. It is old and falling apart. Mice and spiders live in the walls. I haven't seen any yet, but I know it's tick season. With the smallest itch, the slightest tickle, I am convinced insects are invading my body.

Saturday: At 5 a.m. I get up quickly. I don't want to lie in bed any longer. Drinking coffee sounds more inviting than twisting between the sheets.

We hit Lake Pokegama today and float over the long stretch of water. There is no relief from the cold morning winds. I notice my fingers have turned from a soft pink to white. Numbness sets in. The fish are not biting. I don't complain. I just tuck my fingers under my thighs and think how wonderful this day is. I'm not vacuuming the living room or scrubbing my kitchen floor. I'm not putting in extra hours at the office.

This Saturday is perfect. The cold morning gives way to a balmy afternoon, and we peel off layers of jackets and sweatshirts. Kevin is deemed Fisher-God for the day. He has caught walleye, large-mouth bass and northern pike. I scowl at him as I drop yet another tiny perch back in the lake.

Being dedicated anglers, we disregard the dark storm clouds until they are directly overhead. Now we have to reach land before lightning hits the lake and turns us into smoking cinders. At full throttle we go fast enough for the rain to hurt our skin. Kevin's body is tight and erect, face forward, with only his sunglasses for protection. He does not duck down to hide from the rain that pours off his face. I hide my face in my shirt.

Sunday: We are fishing again, this time on Big Rice Lake at a sunken island thirteen feet below the boat. We use a live bait setup today, huge sucker minnows, steel leaders, and big red and white bobbers. This is lazy fishing for the big ones. I cast my line and relax with the sway of the boat. I stare at the shoreline, trying to engrave the water and birch into my memory. I want to recall it on a winter day or when I am lonely, like Wordsworth and his daffodils.

Ten minutes later, my bobber begins to move against the drift of the water. I start to reel in the slack. Kevin tells me to be patient, to make sure the fish takes it before I make my move. I listen to him because he is the Fisher-God. When the bobber goes underwater and remains for many seconds, I bring the pole up hard to the right using both hands. The other end of the line answers back with rapid tugs. My laughing scream bounces off the water. I reel in, finding it difficult to finish the job. Kevin ends my struggle by netting the large-mouth bass at the end of my line. He snaps a picture of my sunburned, smiling face above the five-pounder.

I feel like one of those guys on TV who fish for a living. I float Mr. Bass on the water's surface, holding his belly and jaw for a moment before letting go. He swims away giving one last splash from his tail that sends a spray of lake-water to my face. It's his way of thanking me for letting him live another day.

Sunset. It fills the western sky with hues of orange and pink blending through spiderweb clouds. This is my photo opportunity, alone, on the dock. The lake is calm. Loons break the silence with their mournful cries. I wonder what they're thinking when they split the evening air with a sound so haunting and sad.

When the sun is gone, we drink beer and play cards for shots of tequila. Now that the sky is as black as the lake bottom, I will no longer use the outhouse. I am afraid of critters I cannot see. I squat in the grass just out of range of the cabin lights. The night is so dark I am unable to see if my shoes are getting wet.

Monday: It is the last full day of our weekend retreat. By this time our bodies are dirty, smelly, oily. Without running water, the easiest thing to do is grab a bar of soap, a bottle of shampoo, and jump into the lake. But it is only May, and I am not interested in a cold blasting shock to my system. I fill a giant kettle full of water from the pump outside and warm it on the stove. Using a washcloth I clean my body.

Our weekend retreat near Grand Rapids

My matted hair is another story. Kevin agrees to wash it for me. I sit in a lawn chair in the yard and tilt my smiling head back so he can begin. The warm water rolls down my head through tangles of hair. I can hear it plopping against the earth below and imagine small specks of dirt hitting his ankles. It is a treat to be pampered by someone I love instead of giving money to a woman with a license to beautify.

During any business day I am downtown Minneapolis. My shoulders bump into strangers who move as fast as I do through crowded skyways. Out on the lake we have the place to ourselves. Every minute stretches long across the water. When we do see other people it surprises us. Intruders we call them, as we raise a hand in greeting.

When we return to the cabin, I head toward the outhouse. Kevin has it easy without indoor plumbing. In the outhouse I swat mosquitoes away from my thighs until I am finished and try not to think about the ray of sunlight shining into the pit from a corroded hole in the wall below. I pull my shorts back up calculating the pain of snakebite to exposed skin. Distracted, I almost forget to return the toilet paper to its proper position. I place it in the mouse-free metal bread box and slide its door into place.

When it is time to clean the crappies, I take the last part of the job because I don't want to cut into the creatures when they are still alive and view their steaming insides. I take the broken, gutless bodies as Kevin drops them on the cleaning table before me. Using a filet knife, I slice against the skin and remove the meat. My fingertips hold down the tail of the fish as I cut. My filets end up very thin before I perfect the technique. When I am finished, I use earth-cooled water to rinse away transparent fish scales that have lodged beneath my fingernails.

The time comes when we must leave behind our lazy demeanor, this existence that comes so naturally. We have to prepare for the future that will make us lock the cabin door and fold our bodies back into hard vehicles. We each tackle a chore. We vacuum, make the bed, crush beer cans, bury fish guts, and wash dishes. Our faces are long, focused on our tasks. We don't speak. In our minds we have already left.

Kimberly Mark publishes a literary magazine, **Metal Scratches**, *in Forest Lake.*

Poop and Coop, Inc.
By Betsy Leach

This story begins with a manure pile. Well, actually, it begins long before the manure pile, when my sister was a teenager and worked at a horse-riding stable, and I had a best friend whose parents owned a farm. Those experiences must have been the ultimate cause in setting this story in motion. But the proximate cause for what happened is the manure pile. So we begin with a manure pile and end with butchering fifty-six chickens, a sleep deficit, and a cash flow problem.

Ten years ago, when my sister was in her mid-forties, she and her husband moved from their inner city neighborhood to a farm forty miles from town. Mid-life crisis? Maybe. Who am I to say? But they moved to this farm, which was being divvied up for development, in order to raise horses and, in dream-like anticipation, to raise money.

It turns out my sister had always dreamed of owning horses, and in her mid-forties she somehow decided she wanted to fulfill that dream by going into business breeding and selling horses for big bucks. Now, my sister is a librarian. So is her husband. How this qualified them to become horse breeders, I'm not quite sure, but I think that's where the crisis part of mid-life crisis comes in. Just don't quote me on that.

Anyway, this farm they bought had a manure pile by the pole barn. It was a well-composted manure pile because I don't think the previous owners had had animals for a while. Plus, they'd been farmers all their lives, and they knew what they were doing.

As my sister began collecting horses, and the horses were bred, that manure pile began to grow. Slowly at first when there weren't many horses – and then, well, faster.

As she and her husband settled into their living-on-the-farm-and-commuting-into-town-each-day-to-work existence, my sister's dreams began to shift a bit. They shifted in the direction of the wouldn't-it-be-nice-if-we-could-quit-our-jobs-and-live-off-the-land dream, brought on, I suspect, by the fact that horses take a lot of care, by which I mean, they produce a lot of manure. Producing a lot of manure means their stalls need to be mucked out a lot. My sister and her husband, and her children, and the neighbor's children all spent, and continue to spend, a lot of time, frankly, shoveling shit.

So the manure pile began to grow, and my sister dreamt of using this manure as compost to grow vegetables. These vegetables, of course, would feed her family, reduce her need for money to buy groceries, allow her to quit her job, work with the horses, and give her time to sleep – the "wouldn't it be nice" dream. So she started a garden.

But let me digress a moment and talk about this sleep issue.

Sleep is important in this story too, because the thing about raising horses and growing vegetables and managing manure piles, and commuting eighty miles a day and working full time, is that each takes a lot of time. And all of them together don't leave much time for sleep. So my sister was chronically sleep-deprived, the result of which was that suddenly she wasn't just dreaming of a money-making enterprise, communing with animals and eating home-grown organic foods, but she slipped, I think, into hallucinating about a money-free existence, and forgot about the limits of what is humanly possible.

Before any of us realized the sleep-deprived, hallucinatory nature of her grand schemes, I was enticed into this enterprise. Please understand that I still live in the inner city, forty miles away from my sister's farm. But when I joined her I had just lost a job at the University. I had lots of time on my hands and the need of fresh air, vigorous exercise, work that didn't involve an academic mindset, and the need to feel like I was contributing to the economic survival of my family. So these factors seemed to qualify me as a gardening expert. It started off that my sister and I would plan, plant, weed, and harvest, but pretty quickly I was doing this myself because about this time my sister decided to go into raising chickens, and she took a second job to help pay for upkeep on the horses.

The horse business continued but wasn't bringing in money as quickly as my sister wanted, so she decided that if she had enough chickens she could sell eggs. And the money from the eggs would cover the costs of feeding the chickens and then some. The chicken business would be a self-supporting enterprise and the "then some" could be used to finance the "money-free existence" she dreamed of – or at least the job-free part of it. Of course, what she didn't realize is that no one ever got rich selling eggs, especially when that someone is working more than full-time at jobs forty miles away from the chickens, while she is also trying to garden and maintain horses. Selling anything requires marketing, distributing, accounting, not to mention the fact that eggs don't come ready to sell. They need to be washed once they are collected after they have been laid, once the chickens have been fed and watered. You get the picture. All of this takes time, reducing the time for sleep and increasing the likelihood of ongoing hallucinations.

So I started selling and delivering eggs to people in town. This was fine at first, but then my sister didn't have time to wash eggs, so I added that task to my list of responsibilities that involved commuting eighty miles to the farm to work on the garden and pick up eggs to sell, drumming up customers and delivering the goods.

One more thing about my sister – she has a really soft spot in her heart for animals. Soft to the point where the thought of killing an animal is a horror to her. Or at least it was. And the thought of caging chickens isn't so pleasant either. Now, don't get me wrong – kindness to animals is an admirable quality, but chickens don't continue to lay eggs forever. However, they do continue to eat and require tending as long as they live. And, as it turns out, well-cared for, much loved chickens live a very long time. So this, "they'll pay for themselves" model doesn't quite apply.

And the thing about free-ranging chickens is that they find freshly dug, well-composted garden plots strongly magnetic. Well-composted, organically maintained and pesticide free gardens are full of worms and bugs. And chickens scratch the ground to eat these delicacies. And well-mulched gardens seem an awful lot like perfect nesting sites to them. Chickens simply see things growing in the garden as impediments to their efforts to get at the bugs and worms, or to create a comfy spot to nest.

So, long and short of it is that the chicken thing and the gardening thing, at least the way my sister envisioned them, are largely incompatible. And long-lived chickens who no longer produce eggs cut into not only the "then some" of money earned, but into the money that simply keeps the chickens fed.

My sister decided we should start raising meat chickens to bring in enough money to cover the costs of maintaining the egg-laying-chickens' old-folks-home. If you notice the irony of raising meat chickens as a way out of killing the over-the-hill egg-layers, you aren't the first, but this inconsistency was lost on my sister.

According to her, these enterprises of raising meat and egg chickens required that we build mobile chicken pens to house both the meat and egg-laying chickens – the humane way of raising them. Being a librarian, my sister had read somewhere that if you housed your chickens in these moveable pens, the chickens could get the benefits of ranging over grassy areas, would stay out of the garden, and the chicken manure would fertilize your pastures or fallow garden plots. It is a system that sort of makes your already existing horse manure pile obsolete. And I just want to note that this system also requires people to move the chickens, their pens, their feed and their water around the farm rather than having the food and water in one convenient location and letting the chickens move themselves.

The other thing is, meat chickens are bred to grow fast, which means they have to eat a lot. And eating a lot has two consequences: number one, someone needs to feed them, often because they don't feed themselves, and two, they produce a lot of manure. By the time these chickens are ready to eat, you're ready to kill them – as despicable as that may seem to be if you're like my sister, or if you have no idea what's involved in raising the food that you eat. It's a simple fact. At some point time runs out and it all has to stop.

I'm proud of my sister, I really am. And I envy her ability to keep dreaming even though she never sleeps. I have a freezer full of chickens who lived a blessed life, enough eggs to keep me in omelets, custard and fine cakes from here to eternity, and a shelf full of canned tomatoes left from last year's harvest while this year's plants are flowering and setting fruit. I also have a bank account that is seriously depleted of funds –capital investments in this whole endeavor. Yes, you have to spend money to make money, and yes, nothing good comes without work. But geez!

If you increase inputs to a system, the output is going to increase. And if you add parts to a machine, it requires more energy to run. I think there's some law of physics that controls all this and sends these systems and machines spiraling into chaos unless humans put on the brakes. Just from a human point of view, one person can only do so much in one day without sleep. And we all know that sleep deprived people have slow reaction times when it comes to slamming on the brakes. There is no golden egg to be laid by these chickens. And horses just aren't up to the task.

So pardon me while I head off to rustle up customers for eggs and poultry, and then settle in for a long nap. I hear my sister is contemplating going into business bagging and selling manure. We seem to have an endless supply.

The hobby farm between Scandia and Forest Lake

Betsy Leach is a community organizer for a St. Paul neighborhood. She is married and the mother of two grown sons, the younger of whom took the accompanying photograph

Albert Lea Country Club: Goodbye to All That
By Dex Westrum

On my first visit back to Albert Lea after I heard the Country Club golf course was going to be destroyed, I took my 7-year-old son, Clayton Lyle, for a walk on the old holes 7, 8, and 9. Stakes all over the landscape marked what I assumed were planned housing sites. "This is where I was a little boy and where I was a high school kid," I told him. I tried to explain what the holes looked like in the 1950s and '60s and that the course had been one of the most distinctive nine-hole layouts in Minnesota. It had small greens, narrow fairways, and sand traps you could get lost in. I never saw the additional nine or played any version of the course since the final high school meet of the 1963 season against Red Wing.

"This is a nice course, Dad," Clayton said, "They shouldn't be closing it." What I saw wouldn't have prompted me to call it a nice course. Everything seemed shaved, all the grass was cut to a uniform length, and a lot of the trees had been removed. When my dad, Lyle Westrum, was pro-greenkeeper there in 1960 and 1961, he let the grass between the fairways grow into a challenging rough. Everything had a more wild and sublime feel to it. You had to hit the ball straight. If you hit it crooked, you had to be a shot maker to get the ball out of the tall grass and back into play.

In fact, the long grass on the slope between the ninth tee and the second fairway gave me one of my more harrowing moments. I was changing the water sprinklers on the greens shortly after midnight, driving around the course in the 1948 vintage club pickup. I decided to get to the eighth green from the second green via the slope and had to take the slope at a sort of 45-degree angle. I started out fine but the grass was long, dewy, and slippery. The truck slid toward a five-foot drop-off into number 2 fairway. Slamming on the brakes just made the truck slide faster. I was sure I was going to roll, and my father was not a patient man. How was I going to explain that I had wrecked the club's truck? But the truck came to the drop-off and slid right down, leaving itself and me upright.

My earliest Country Club memory is of a wad of mud on the back of my right hand. I was 3 years old and had been stung by a bee. When my father returned from World War II, he got a job with the Albert Lea Fire Department and joined the Country Club, where he had been a caddy and pro shop assistant as a youth. The day of the bee sting, he was playing against Arleigh Miller in the finals of the 1948 club championship. The match was even after the required 36 holes, and Dad lost on the third extra hole when Miller holed a wedge from off the green for a birdie on number 3. I have no idea if anyone except my mother knew I had been stung by a bee, or if I cried; all I can see in my mind is that wad of mud.

The highlight of every summer was the Fourth of July because the Country Club was where the fireworks were shot off. The whole town turned out, cars lining old Highway 13, along number 3, and the driveway, along number 4. People sat elbow to elbow on number 7 hill. My dad and another fireman would drive a fire engine onto the golf course through an opening by Edgewater Park and stop at the bottom of number 7 hill to set off the fireworks. Best of all, there was free ice cream for all the kids. I don't remember if the ice cream came from Morlea or Thomson Dairy, but it was rich and it was cold—and one dip was plenty. The next morning the caddies would find cardboard remnants of the fireworks; sometimes they found them in the bushes by the clubhouse. One year there was a bunch of the stuff on the clubhouse roof.

That Edgewater was so close to number 7 provided my father with a challenge on the morning after the high school prom in 1961. He was in the pickup whipping the dew off the greens so they could be mowed when he discovered two naked teenage lovers sleeping on number 7 green. Fortunately, he was more than a hundred yards away when he first saw them. He didn't want to embarrass them or himself, so he went back to the pro shop, picked up his wedge and practice ball bag, and returned to hit balls at them from a safe distance until they woke up and ran off.

Even though he kept his job at the fire department, my father became the Country Club professional in 1952. Golf was a new phenomenon for average Americans in the early '50s, and the demand for lessons was high. Firemen were off duty every other day, and Dad would put in from six to twelve hours on the lesson tee. There were no driving ranges in those days, no practice balls that could be hit and left lying on the ground.

Lesson balls had to be shagged, and I was elected to stand in the practice fairway collecting balls in a shag bag while the pupils took aim at me. Once in a while I would lose sight of a ball in the sun and get hit, but fortunately most pupils couldn't hit the ball straight until the lesson was nearly over. I received forty cents for a half hour lesson, which resulted in quite a sum by the end of the day. I immediately spent half of my earnings at the Ben Franklin store on new comic books. I eventually had more than three hundred comics, which my mother threw away shortly after I left for college.

In those days one important source of income for a golf pro was club storage. Members would pay to have their clubs kept there and looked after. On the days my father was at the fire department, my mother and I would wash over two hundred sets. We would gently take the white ball marks off the hackers' woods with steel wool and clean the grooves of all the irons with a tee. During these days I got to know Rollie Friday, the club manager. Rollie was one of the nicest guys I ever knew. He was always smiling and upbeat. Some days I would work alone, and if there were other kids around, we could get to goofing off and Rollie would have to scold us. I never liked being scolded, but I always liked Rollie.

During this time, Dick Davies Jr. and I played a few holes of golf because our fathers were trying to interest us in the game. We weren't interested because we had to hit the ball too often. We were just too young. Dick Jr. never did become what we would call an avid golfer. Even when he was one of the best players on the high school team, he rarely toured the links in the summertime. He worked for my dad in the morning cutting the greens and then retired to his sailboat on Fountain Lake in the afternoons. I worked in the pro shop then and usually could squeeze in nine holes in the early afternoon, but could never get Dick to stay and play.

Dick Davies, Sr. was one of my favorite people. Most club members treated me as if I were invisible or a personal servant, but when he came into the shop, he always asked what I was up to or how I had been playing. He liked to tell me about swing changes he was making. He loved to hit balls in the early mornings before going to work at his realty agency. I can still see him in the glistening dew pounding ball after ball working on what became a superior and dependable swing. He was the first player I ever saw employ the pre-shot routine that was eventually made popular by Jack Nicklaus. On the tee, he would stand behind the ball looking down the fairway and adjust his grip. Then, keeping his eye on the spot he wanted to hit, he would walk up to the ball, clear this throat, and swing. It seemed to work for him and Jack. Both won a lot of tournaments in their respective careers.

Dad became pro at the Faribault Golf and Country Club in 1957, but I returned to Albert Lea to caddy for my uncle, Bumper Westrum, in the Albert Lea Shortstop of 1959. Based largely on his record as a junior player, where we won everything from two state high school championships to the amateur division of the PGA's St. Paul Open, Bumper was still regarded as one of the best, if not *the* best player in Southern Minnesota. He moved through the first three matches without a hiccup and was narrowly defeated by Al Lerum in the finals.

The Albert Lea Shortstop was a major event in our family. Uncle Bud won it before he gave up the game. Dad came in second before he turned pro, and Bumper was winner and runner-up before he turned pro. Uncle Bill made it to the semi-finals before he left town for California. With the destruction of the old course, one of the longest continuous amateur golf tournaments in Minnesota has come to an end.

Dad left the Country Club after the 1961 season and took a job in the Twin Cities, but we kept our home in Albert Lea so I had two more springs on the old course as a member of the Albert Lea High School golf team. My teammates were Davies, Dick Jones, John Hurst, Gary Plante, and John Ingebritson. Jones was by far the best player, winning the state championship in 1962 and the Big Nine Conference title in 1961 and 1963. He often claimed medalist honors in dual meets with scores near or below par.

The rest of us were capable of breaking 40 on the old course so we were a formidable lot. In fact, I don't think we ever lost a home match. The hard-to-hit greens, the yawning sand traps, and the up and down stances required of our hilly fairways were probably too much for visiting teams.

All this is running through my head when Clayton says, "Why don't they make it a public course?" He's insightful for a 7-year-old, but I don't think he's ready for a discussion of the real and imagined class distinctions that were delineated by membership in the Albert Lea Country Club over the years.

"I think somebody tried that," I said. "But they kept the clubhouse private. You have to understand that for lots of people belonging to the Country Club had nothing to do with valuing the golf course. If it had, we wouldn't be looking at all these stakes."

Dick Davies Jr. watches Dex Westrum blast from the number 6 sand trap at the Albert Lea Country Club in 1963.

Dex Westrum, who lived in Albert Lea and Faribault, teaches literature and film at the Milwaukee Center of Upper Iowa University. His mother, Marian Porter Westrum, also contributed a story to this volume.

Snow Angels
By Amanda Elizabeth Haldy

"Minnesota is now officially in a new hardiness zone," Mom said just the other day. She glowed like a furnace where she stood over the kitchen table, fueled up with the latest details of our strange weather.

"Oh?" I leaned forward, eager for any incriminating evidence pointing to climate change. I was sure that something was wrong with the weather, and that global warming wasn't science fiction, or years away, but right outside the door. "So you mean the plants are changing or something?"

"It means that the yearly average is enough degrees warmer that we can plant different seeds. Different growing season—like a region more south of us would've been." I was edging through a half-baked winter beside my parents, in their home in Becker. I hoped it would be my last year before taking to the skies and leaving the nest empty at last. I was old enough that it was embarrassing to tell strangers where I lived. My two brothers were already gone. I was the poorest one—and it didn't help that I wasn't dating someone with a reliable income. That was our situation: Mom, Stepdad Rusty, two little Labradors, and me.

December I baked dozens of cookies in preparation: pfeffernuesse, sugarplums, mincemeat foldovers, teacakes, gingerbread men… I steamed a figgy pudding and wrapped it in brandy-soaked cheesecloth to ripen for a day and a half before Christmas Eve, when we would ignite a ladle full of brandy and drizzle blue flames over the final treat of the night. Everyone was coming to my mother's house for the holiday. I had completed all my shopping and suited up the packages in brown paper and colored foil and adorned them with real satin ribbons—all within a day of the tree going up. And what a tree it was.

Twelve feet tall it stood shimmering under the vaulted roof like a golden idol, a Roman trophy bejeweled with glass and candy and stars. The pagan roots of the Christmas tree seemed to spread through the house, wall to wall, like a vibration, redoubling into a harmonic. It made you feel pretty sure it was almost Christmas. I wanted this one, my last one at home, to be quintessential. I wanted to distill it to remain pure in my memory—firm, warm, absolutely itself—so that the memory would become an almost tangible thing I could carry with me wherever I went. I would have this Minnesota Christmas inside me when I left to live in a warmer state.

However, the winter part was missing. It was in the forties with not a drop of snow. "I kind of like it," Mom answered my complaint. "I certainly don't miss driving in a bunch of icy muck."

"But this is unnatural!" I said, "It's one thing if you live in a subtropical climate, but this is unheard of for Minnesota."

"Maybe you won't have to move south then." I suspected she wanted me to live with her forever. She liked having someone around to entertain the dogs and keep them fed. Maybe she even liked having me around.

As Christmas drew nearer, I began to pray. I prayed when I was in my car for that's when the trouble was most obvious. During my commute to work, I passed rows of skeletal trees with a miserly grip on the last of their tattered brown leaves. Plains of parched grass unrolled everywhere I looked, and the desolate ruts between the roads followed me for miles, even after I had gone indoors. It had been a very long November.

We had a bitter October, all scourging north winds and blights of frost. The leaves turned and scattered like worthless banknotes. That was October-November. Then we had November-November, which was a paragon of the bleak month itself. Now, it was December-November, a withered brown hand stretching toward the holidays as if a month could have a grudge. So as I sat in my car, piloting along in silence but for the radio pronouncing the names of my fears—endangered, climate change, ice caps, and drought—I prayed. "Please, God," I said, "let it snow. You know I'm not one for winter, so surely if I am asking for this, the situation must be bad."

The day before Christmas Eve, it snowed. I had everything ready, my hair set for curls the next day, and food to feed my family for hours, and it snowed. It wasn't cold enough to have a fire and roast chestnuts, but you can't ask for so much. When I looked out the kitchen window and saw the lace of snowfall over the trees, such a peace filled me up and made me light, as if my soul was a balloon that could sail up to become a part of the sky. "It's beginning to look a lot like Christmas," I said as I pointed out the window.

"We'll see if it amounts to a hill of beans," replied my ever-pragmatic mother. Evening the next day, our stomachs bloated from my month-long efforts, Mom, Uncle, Cousin and I went out to walk off our stupor. The smell of snow, clean and mineral, is unlike any other. The green of a pine looks like an entirely different color against white, richer and somehow warmer, established by the snow the way night lends warmth to distant houselights.

The potency of any season is in its contrast to the others, and what contrasts winter more keenly than its sleep of snow? As we walked and talked about weather and work, our feet made blue-lined stamps alongside the tracks of deer and foxes. There wasn't a "hill of beans" to be sure, but there was enough to paint over the dirt and decay of the past three months. There was enough to look like a Jane Austen Christmas. I could imagine carriages cutting wet lines along the road and ladies' slippers whisking carefully up the front steps. If you stepped lightly enough, the snow wouldn't come over your toes. Rejoicing in my secret knowledge that someone had answered my prayers, I felt it was just the right amount.

Over the next two or three days, the snow faded back into the earth. We would have to make do with a brown New Years, and that was fine. So I thought, until my stepdad, Rusty, reminded me. I had completely forgotten in the midst of the festivities that my step-nephews (to coin the term) were coming up to visit, along with my stepbrother and his wife. I had never met his family before.

"I would really like for them to have snow while they're here," Rusty muttered one evening. "These kids have never seen snow before." He was sitting on the couch in front of the TV, not watching it. He stared out through the walls, deliberate, driven by either the pain from his back injury or the pain of grandchildren without snow. "I remember one winter," he said, "we got a blizzard with about five feet of snow or something. I just remember walking down the road—in those days parents let their kids wander wherever the heck—and it was minus forty. I'm out there with my friends, walking down Main Street, and we're kicking the antennas of cars. The snow was so deep we were walking on top of cars, kicking antennas just because we could."

Yes, I thought. Yes, That's a Minnesota winter. I remembered mountainous drifts wedged against the house, helped by shovelfuls from the driveway. The piles were so high by mid January I could have climbed them to the roof. When was the last time you saw snow like that?

"We're lucky we didn't fall in," Rusty laughed. "Eventually, when the parents heard on the radio how cold it was, they came and got us."

"I'm surprised they even did that much," Mom chimed in from the kitchen. "I'm surprised they didn't just open the door and yell, "Hey kid! Get back here!"

Every Minnesota child should have the chance to pit his or her life against the elements. Something good comes of the prolonged darkness and unforgiving cold, the eggshell landscapes. It builds character. Take my stepfather. He is an excellent Minnesotan. He's thrown his back out three times but still works ten-hour days, and he never complains when Mom asks him to take care of household repairs. "Football is on, you know," he said once, but he quickly corrected it with, "yes, dear."

Such patience and passivity in the face of suffering comes from Minnesota winters. Subzero weather keeps us tempered. The snow trickling down our collars, ice crust on our cars every morning, these keep us realistic. Kids these days seem materialistic and needy for entertainment because we haven't had any good, solid winters for a while. They ought to have to stand at the end of the block waiting for the school bus as the wind forms ice crystals in their eyelashes and sprays the snow like shrapnel. Such an experience changes your perspective.

Rusty didn't have to say another word; I was with him. My stepnephews needed snow. They needed affirmation in their father's roots, where they came from, and the kind of strength that lived secretly in their genes. They deserved memories like their father had of snow. But what were the chances I could get it to snow again?

I took to praying in my car again. "Please, God," I said, "I know I am asking a lot, and you already granted my wish once… but this time it's for the children." Each night, as their arrival crept nearer, my pleading began to taste a little more like desperation. "Please, God. Let there be snow for the children."

My step-nephews arrived in a barren scrubland; my automobile prayers had not borne fruit. To add to my desperation, the more I came to know my three step-nephews, the more certain I was that they needed snow. The infant could probably live without it. He was a good sleeper, which suggested he could get through the winter without the diversion, but the 2-year-old was another story. He didn't care for sleep and never sat still for more than a half hour, and then only when plunked in front of *Curious George*. He needed rescuing from rerun purgatory, and he needed something else to put in his mouth besides the toys of our tormented dogs. What fun he would have eating snow! We could tell him about the yellow snow later, and then maybe he would leave the poor dogs alone. Then there was Esai, the 9-year-old. "He was really looking forward to seeing snow," said his mother. "I promised him snow."

"Hello! How are you?" Esai proclaimed then smiled as if embarrassed by the volume of his own voice, hiding behind his juice cup. The cup displayed the Superman shield, and launching from the snap-on lid was a plastic Superman himself, heroic arms wrapped around an accordion straw.

"Cool cup," I said. I wanted him to feel at ease, maybe even make him smile.

"Thank you!" he spoke with overwhelming politeness, like one learning a foreign language who had memorized certain intonations.

"Esai has autism," Mom told me several times in advance. I wasn't sure what to expect. I saw a very sweet boy with a lot of energy that he kept to himself. I could almost hear his private world buzzing around him, like fragments of music from someone else's headphones.

"I just want him to make it through school, and to make friends," Veri said when Esai left the room.

"He doesn't have any friends?" I couldn't believe it. He looked too happy to be friendless. But he knew all the songs on the radio and could name every performer. Kids think music is cool. How could he not have friends?

I wanted more than ever for Esai to have snow. He would gain something—a memory—that would stay with him even after the snow had melted. It would be something none of the other kids in Georgia had. Esai would be truly cool. The kid who had snow over winter break. He wouldn't have any trouble finding friends then. That night, I thought about kneeling down beside my bed to make a formal proposal to God on Esai's behalf. But I forgot. I was already in bed with the lights out, warm and sleepy, before I remembered it. The next day was New Years Eve.

Instead of praying, I thought about polar bears. I thought about whether this was really climate change or just El Nino. Or was El Nino on the prowl because of climate change? Perhaps this eerie warm weather was a sign of the coming apocalypse. More importantly, was all of this our own doing, or something inevitable in the science of planet earth? Soft sadness crept over me as I realized how fragile our perceived world actually is. To think that something we have so long experienced as completely dependable—the climate, the place we live on this earth, our home—can die or adapt like an old tradition. Change is hard.

The next morning, the sound of singing awakened me. The voice was melodic, perfectly tuned and rhythmic. This didn't sound like a kid singing, but it was Esai. He was singing along with *Curious George*, and snow was flickering in the forest. Wishes have a way of coming true at inconvenient times. I was beginning to regret my fervent piety as New Years Eve found me driving to work in a mess of rain-turning-to-ice-turning-to-snow. I passed three cars in the ditch as I pelted along at a full 20 mph down the highway.

I was an hour late, nerves fried and hands cramped from clutching the wheel. It's a good thing, I reminded myself. Keeps us realistic. I couldn't help but feel a little bounce in my step, too. If this kept up, Esai could build a snowman in the front yard. Humming "Frosty the Snowman," I made it home in time to set up the New Years snacking smorgasbord. There were perhaps three inches already, and it was still snowing. The real fun, however, wouldn't happen until the next day, in the light, when the kids could go out and play. We were long past the days when parents let their children wander around in blizzards.

New Years morning looked truly new. Still snowing, the day was a field of white velvet trees. It wasn't the foot-upon-foot I remembered from my childhood, when winter storms were the norm, but it covered the ground and the woodpiles, and made the tree limbs look as delicate as porcelain. It was enough to elicit a territorial thrill to be the first one to make tracks over its back, and enough to make the sloping expanses with no tracks at all look sacred.

Esai was sitting beside the Christmas tree, watching cartoons. Every once in a while, he glanced at the flakes trickling down just past the window. I was proud of our little show—also wondering why Esai wasn't out there right now, dashing through the forest. He could be experiencing the flakes dancing over his cheeks, catching in his hair. I stopped at the window. "Well! Look at that." I glanced at Esai. He kept his eyes shyly on the TV as if I wasn't talking specifically to him. "It's still snowing!"

I was busy that day, afraid I would miss the kids in the snow, but finally as I came back in from an errand, I caught sight of Esai in a thick jacket and borrowed boots. He rolled a ball of snow, packed it with his awkward gloves.

"Esai loves it out there," Mom commented from the kitchen. "He's been out there for hours." What gratification was mine then. Both my prayers and their answers were to a great purpose. There was Esai, through the gateway to the world of imagination (that children too rarely enter nowadays). As he packed snowballs, scraped lines through the blankets on the cars and marched across the yard with his eyes fixed on the impressions left by his treads, I silently urged him to build a snowman, to lie down and make a snow angel. That's what I would do. I could feel the cold blunting my fingers and toes, the raw burn on my cheeks. I heard the crunch of boots. I felt the way packed snow slips under a snowsuit as glib as pure ice.

And I remembered the snow pile climbing up the side of the house and a cave my big brother carved through the pile. It had a door on one end and another in the roof like a submarine port. It was a long, intricate cave, with two rooms shaped like organs—a liver and pancreas inside an ice monster. I remembered hiding in the snow cave, surprised by how warm it could be in a house of ice, squealing, flailing over drifts that swallowed my legs up to the knee, and the thud of snowballs against my padded coat.

I know why I wanted Esai to have snow. It wasn't for him that I wanted it. In my dreaming heart, I wanted him to have snow like I did, like his father did and his father's father, because then I could remember one more time what it was like to be a Minnesota child in the winter.

Little Amanda, her brother and dad in the snow.

Amanda Haldy, who lives in Becker, writes fiction and poetry and works as a freelance copywriter. She has been published in various magazines such as **Rain Taxi** *and* **13 Minutes**.

Travels with my South Minneapolis Softball Gang
By Dennis Stern

In 1983 when every beer joint in South Minneapolis had a men's softball team, I was manager of the 5404 Club's hard-drinking aggregation. It wasn't like the Crips vs. the Bloods gangs, but competition between teams in those days got pretty intense. I liked my team so much I quit a good night job as a singing waiter at the Friars Dinner Theater so I could continue to play left field for the 5404. The combination of slow pitch softball and beer drinking was like a religion, and we were its followers.

5404 was the address of the bar on Minnehaha Avenue where country music twanged and beer flowed freely. Several of our players, mostly tradesmen, sang and played electric guitar in a group. Pool tables sat between the stage and a large lacquered oak bar. Although I saw a good fight or two, the only one I participated in was while trying to break up a skirmish between two ladies–a barmaid and a blonde softball player. All the males wanted to see this cat fight so I caught some grief about my peacemaking effort. I got a well-deserved punch on the jaw, as one of the ladies hit me instead of her adversary. Oh, we had good times.

Norm Comstock, owner of the bar, encouraged me to set up as many "beer games" and tournaments as possible to help business. "I'll even pay you," he said. I didn't need that. We enjoyed 96 games one year–most were beer games played at a local park, and the winning team brought the losing team to its bar. Norm was happy with the people and the profits.

The occasional out-of-town tournament was fun for everyone. The little town of Ivanhoe is located about three and a half hours southwest of Minneapolis, and the residents always celebrate Polska Kielbasa Days in early August. My Eastern European taste buds salivated at the thought of the festival food. Someone suggested that our team rent a 19-passenger bus, bring the wives and girlfriends, and camp out in Ivanhoe for the weekend. It hadn't rained in that area for six weeks, so the weather looked good. We assembled at the 5404 about 4 on Friday afternoon. We loaded sleeping bags, tents, even a camp stove, and lots of beer into a Dodge van I purloined–and was responsible for. We couldn't wait to strut our stuff on the field.

In good spirits and anticipating a great weekend, our bunch of characters packed into that van. One of the players was Roddy Blue, a redneck from North Dakota, who played as hard as he swore. Roddy had a top tooth missing, was gritty and could run well for someone almost 30. He liked picking on Rick Felix, one of our two native American players. Rick was a great young shortstop – lanky, witty and well-liked by everyone. Although some on the team kidded me, complained about my managing and called me "teacher," Rick didn't. He was an "in" guy on the team, and considerate to others and their wives.

Others on the team included Dicky Fiddler, Lowell Nelson, Freddy Milhanek, Chris Lerner, Gordy Lerner and Georgie Anderly. Georgie loved to clown, but could show courage. Once in the 5404, as a fill-in bartender, he disabled a threatening customer with a knife. Georgie blocked a punch, the knife fell, and his counter blow sent the stranger flying over a pool table. Georgie and the barmaid subdued the guy until the police came.

Doc Springer was my closest friend on the team and co-manager. He always wore a cap to hide his thinning hair, and he always sipped warm coffee from a thermos when driving his old Impala Chevy. Doc, about 280 pounds, had hands large as maul hammers. He always told a good story. One of my favorites was how it took himself, his brother and father to pull in an enormous catfish near Boscobel, Wisconsin. He could crunch home runs, bowl 240, hustle in pool games and play a mean game of horseshoe. But what I liked best was that of all the people I had ever met, no one was better at making others–strangers included–feel good. It was a great gift.

Other players were Scott Smith, Dale Dickson, Mike Stephens and Dave Olson. Dave was a blond, well built Norseman who came on the trip with his wife, Gina. Swede Johansen, a good friend of Stephens, was along just to watch. I was the driver, and the sun filled my eyes as we headed west on the highway. "Turn the radio on that country station, Denny," somebody hollered. I complied.

This was going to be fun. We had camped many times before in the Graceville, Lake Traverse area in western Minnesota, but this was new for us. Everyone usually drove their individual cars on trips.

Minnesota Memories 7

It got dark early as clouds started to fill the sky. We had no cell phones in those days, so no one could tell us as we drove southwest that a huge rainstorm had hit Ivanhoe. The softball tourney was washed out. The call reached the 5404 a half hour after we left. Our van ran into the rain on the road, but we hoped we could still play ball. We kept driving, and everybody kept drinking–except me, the designated driver.

We got to the bar in Ivanhoe, The Ale House, sponsor of the tourney, about 7:30. Rain was coming down in sheets, and the bar manager told us the bad news. Spirits plunged. Big Doc, who alternated between pitcher and first base, approached me wearing his drenched cap, wet from sweat and rain. At his size, he could sweat even in cold weather. Doc did most things in a big way. He was worried now. "Whew," Doc whistled. "This could be some trouble. What are we going to do? I think we should consider going back to Minneapolis." He told me he was thinking about the drinking and what could get out of hand. After all, we had a reputation to uphold–as big city guys.

"Well, no way," chorused about four of the players and their wives when they caught wind of our conversation. "We can stay here and have a good time. Maybe the weather will break, and we can do something else," Dicky Fiddler, the pitcher, second baseman and real leader of our team said. He squeezed his loyal wife, Darla, and said calmly to me, "Just hold on, Denny. The night is young." Everybody kept drinking.

A customer opened the door and came into the bar. Rain dripped from the roof down the door frame. But the weather wasn't quite as bad as before. Seven or eight of our team and some strangers went outside with their beer glasses. The fresh cool night air was cleaned by the storm.

Suddenly we heard cursing and turned around to the sound of landing fists. Roddy Blue, the redneck, and Rick Felix were rolling around on the cobblestone street punching each other. Rick had enough of "Indian" teasing. A crowd gathered round and started cheering. The rest of us, full of beverage, strangely just looked on. Some felt the redneck was getting what he deserved. Suddenly, with three quick steps, Doc, my giant friend, went over to the combatants and grabbed Rick's collar. With one hand, he lifted the well-built 180-pounder into the air and sat him down gently.

"This fight is over," he bellered at the top of his voice. Bracing his massive legs, he stretched his arms between the two. Rick eased off into the crowd. Roddy started to moan, holding his head. He slowly got up. The spectators chuckled and went back inside. The brawl was over, but the drinking was just getting started.

About 12:30 a.m. somebody said, "Let's get some breakfast." The idea was to all pile in the van and drive to an all-night diner just outside of town.

"But wait a minute, Georgie is missing," Mike Stephens called out. Georgie got this idea that maybe he could hide somewhere in town, and that we could not leave without him. This would be funny, the prankster thought. We drove down streets and alleys, and after about 30 minutes of searching, found him slinking between two garbage cans behind a feed store. Mike and Freddy helped Georgie get in the bus, and he and some others sat in back. Arriving in the dimly lit parking lot, we filed slowly out of the vehicle and dodged puddles walking into the diner.

"Hey, pretty lady, do you want to go out later?" Georgie slurred to a local woman across the counter from him. He slid off his stool and lay on the floor.

"Better get up, Sunshine," Dicky said to his buddy. Everybody laughed except Doc and the town deputy, who was seated in the corner.

Doc took me aside and said, "We've got to get everybody back home. Something worse is going to happen if we don't act quickly. Someone will get hurt or end up in jail." I listened to this plea as everyone paid their bills and we squeezed into the green Dodge van. The rain had started up again. Adding up the pros and cons, I pointed the van eastward and headed back toward home. Those on the back of the bus, including Dicky and Georgie, fell quickly asleep.

An hour later, we passed through the town of Marshall. Darla, Dicky's wife, woke him up and told him what direction we were going. "Hey, what's going on here?" he yelled. When Doc explained, Dicky said, "Hell, no. We paid for this trip – this weekend – and we are not going back. Stop this bus!"

I hit the brakes, and about six of us piled out into the ditch next to the van. Dicky was pointing his finger at Doc's chest as they both argued–faces about two inches apart. Dicky felt he was sticking up not only for his rights, but for the rights of the majority on the bus. Swede, Mike's friend, was on Doc's side. As a spectator, he had enough of this night of drinking, fighting, cold soaking rain and prankish nonsense. I just hoped that Doc and Dicky, who I considered great friends of mine, would not swing at each other. They did not. It was decided that Doc, Swede and the badly bruised Roddy would get off at Granite Falls just 10 miles ahead, and the rest of us would turn back to Ivanhoe. The bus back to the cities at Granite Falls would not arrive until 4:40 a.m., but Doc and the others didn't care. We dropped them off in the damp darkness at the bus depot.

I turned the bus around and was doing about 50 mph on the two-lane road back to Ivanhoe. At least the fighting had ended, I thought. The strong rain blew horizontally across the road so much that the wipers at full speed could not handle the downfall. I should have stopped. Suddenly, the van edged off the road and hit some ruts. Bump, bump, clump, bump went the van, as sleepers in back were startled by jolts and noise. Somehow I slowed and cranked the wheel, and the van, a chamber of life on wheels, crept back on the blacktop. I had been scared that with so many on board, it all could have ended there. I whispered thanks.

Morning light was peeking behind us from the orangy east as we pulled into a park close to Ivanhoe. It was cold and still raining. Some of us crawled under some picnic tables and got about an hour of broken rest before it was time to go into town. We were shivering severely. We found the field where the cancelled ball tournament was supposed to be held and started to put up our tents. After someone brought hot coffee from the café, we collapsed and napped a little more. Our guys were good at overcoming hangovers. We had a challenge this time.

I visited Dave and Gina and their two little girls in their tent. Gina was okay with staying–at least it appeared so on the surface. Dave asked me, "What do you think about this? Is there someone we could play?" He was referring to one other team from the Cities who we knew was camping at the field. I went to their manager, Red, from the Nic-Lake Bar to talk. He was happy to set up two games between us and a team from Ivanhoe–all for beer, of course.

We would start at 1 p.m. to give the ground a little time to dry out. Some of us scraped little canals with shovels so water could run its way off the field. Puddles about 30 feet wide soon became smaller. After that we headed to Main Street, where Polska Kielbasa Day was going on. The sausages went so good with hot coffee. Saturday town life was in full swing. The barbershop and hardware store were full of farmers smoking pipes and laughing–happy because of the much needed rain.

We headed back to the field. The games were intense and fun as ever. I dived for a ball and came up with my side caked with mud and grass. We lost the first game, but somebody kidded that was on purpose, so we could get to drink the beer wagered on the game while the other two teams had to play.

We won our second game, but our Freddy, running to second base, got his nose busted by an errant throw. The sun came out as we sloshed and slid around in the mud during and after the games. Some of the children skimmed on garbage bags down hills on the still wet grass. Hot dogs and hamburgers smoked on grills. Lawn darts came out, and the guys proved for the hundredth time they were proficient at hand-eye coordination.

We packed our tents and hit the road toward Minneapolis in that green 19-passenger bus and easily covered the 180 miles back home with the red sun setting at our backs. Everybody was happy. Dicky was right in having us stay the weekend. Somehow, as usual, we managed to have a great time.

Late that evening I pulled the bus safely into the 5404's pot-holed, gravel parking lot, and we slowly unpacked. There was a contentment present like nothing bad had ever happened. A good weekend.

We were in another softball tournament the next weekend in the suburbs near Cedar Avenue in the south river bottoms. We won some games, but winning a three-foot-high beer drinking trophy made of empty cans filled us with even more pride. But an amazing thing happened at that valley tournament. Doc hit a huge home run; the force he exerted hurt his neck for years to come. Dicky was the other hitting star with a triple and double. Afterwards, obviously in a good mood, joking, he rested his head in Doc's lap while sipping a beer in the late afternoon's horizontal sunlight, whereas the two had been screaming in each other's faces only a week before. I couldn't have been happier.

It didn't rain that weekend. Everyone drove their own cars. We vowed that day to never again go in a van together to a tournament. We never did. Years passed. This group of aging warriors played ball until our bodies cried "enough." Some of the guys still bowl or play golf together. Our long-loved bar is closed now, the space taken over by a Chinese restaurant.

Rick is now one of America's premiere Indian artists. His paintings hang in university museums in the Northwest and as far away as Munich, Germany. He is married to an author. Doc, who had a profound influence on Rick's life that night in Ivanhoe, passed away in 2003. Sadly, only Mike and I from the team attended his funeral. Maybe there was still some hurt there from that Ivanhoe weekend. But my compadre Doc is probably still breaking up fights, making friends, and telling stories somewhere in a 3.2 joint in the sky.

Dennis Stern, who works in advertising and loves to travel, lives in Mendota Heights with his wife, Mary Lee. He wrote and published **Tips On Playing Slowpitch Softball** *in the 1980s. Now his closest connection to softball is coaching a beep ball team for the blind in the Twin Cities area. He can be reached at dennisstern@comcast.net*

Bean-Walking in Southern Minnesota
By Patricia Kniefel

I grew up in the small town of Sherburn located in southwest Minnesota, near the Iowa border. I was one of eight children, a large family that was not unusual in our area during the 1960s and '70s. I was one of the oldest. Due in part to the large family size, but also to my dad's strong work ethic, my siblings and I were all expected to earn our own money for current and future use. My parents did not have extra cash to hand out for movie theaters and extracurricular activities. If we wanted spending money, we had to work for it on our own, but job opportunities were few and far between.

I was just 8 years old when I started my first job. It would be a job that I worked at during the next fifteen summers of my life. This job was the single most motivating factor that pushed me toward a college degree and pursuit of a "professional" career.

My dad got the summer job for me and my older brother. Dad thought he could help out a farmer friend as well as help his children earn a little money. Dad volunteered our services to walk the farmer's bean fields and pull out weeds. This labor would help the farmer bring in a higher yield from the soybean fields during fall harvest.

My brother and I initially thought this would be a pretty swell job. We had never had a paying job before, so we were a very proud pair walking out the door with our dad that first morning. And we were a pretty sorry sight dragging in the door later that day. We never knew we could walk so far in one day, swing a hoe twice our height for so long, or endure such back-breaking work for so many hours.

I don't recall for sure, but I think this first job lasted for at least a couple of weeks. We got paid by the hour and felt on top of the world when we were handed a wad of green cash as we finished the last acre. We successfully completed our first employment opportunity (along with a great deal of complaining along the way) and were promptly escorted to open a passbook savings account for future needs.

My dad already had a full-time job but felt this was such a good opportunity for us that he would use his vacation time from his real job to walk and clean the fields with us. After several years of experience, he felt comfortable sending us out to the fields without his supervision and appointed one of us the crew chief, earning an extra 50 cents an hour. We would all eventually get the opportunity to learn and use the skills of leading, motivating, and negotiating our own crew members–not always an easy task and sometimes resulting in a corruption of power.

The bean-walking business flourished. It was a hard, dirty job that even some of the farmers' kids weren't required to do. However, our crew grew in size, and the number of jobs increased every year. Eventually, our crew consisted of fifteen people, including my brothers and sisters as well as several kids in the community who proved themselves worthy of the job and had the stamina to endure the labor. It was considered to be a plum position to be on our crew. We made great money, but we worked awfully hard for it. And the workload definitely weeded out the men from the boys and the women from the girls.

We were in the fields at 8 a.m. sharp. Each person brought his or her own hoe, and Dad would hand-sharpen each one every morning. We would line up in an assigned order and head down the rows, chopping or pulling out any weed in front or on either side of us. We were allowed to talk only if we could do it while we worked. We got a 15-minute break at mid-morning and another one at mid-afternoon. We were off for an hour at noon and either ate a sack lunch in the field or drove home for a hot cooked meal if we were working at a farm near home. We then worked until 6 p.m. Our workdays were Monday through Saturday, and we worked from the time the soybean plants were several inches high until they were so large and bushy that we could no longer distinguish rows in the fields–generally from mid-June to mid-August.

I absolutely detested the bean walking season. The six to eight weeks we worked each summer were the longest and hardest times of my young life. It is the very reason why summer is still my least favorite time of year. Those several weeks seemed to last forever. They were a blur of never-ending muscle aches, sunburn blisters on top of sunburn blisters, and utter exhaustion by the end of each day. The never-ending heat and humidity stripped us of all energy and tolerance, and was, without a doubt, the worst part of all. We prayed for storms and rain delays, which were too few and far between. We made excellent money–enough to buy our school clothes for the year and tuck a good amount away for college. However, I would have quit a million times over if I would have been allowed, but Dad refused to listen to our whines and complaints.

In spite of everything, we did have a few good laughs, memorable events, and creative pranks in the bean fields over the years. I recall losing a tennis shoe in the middle of the field when the rain-soaked gooey mud literally sucked my shoe off my foot while we were trudging along. The tennis shoe is now somewhere in China because it was pulled so deep into the earth, we never did find it. We all came home that day covered in mud from feet to hips. Mom took the hose to us outside before she allowed any of us in the house. Of course, there was also initiation into the bean-walking group each year. New crew members would unknowingly get the laces of their shoes tied together while resting during one of the first breaks of the season, and we would all laugh uproariously when they stood up to take a step and went head over heels.

Very heated philosophical discussions occurred between the guys and the girls about who was stronger, smarter, better looking, etc. The girls talked about the romance of their weekend dates, and the guys bragged about their weekend conquests. We also experienced some pretty creative and nasty name-calling/power plays between siblings and co-workers when we would all become irritable from the heat, monotony, and hard work during those long, long days.

Both boys and girls on the crew had to learn to go to the bathroom in the cornfield next door and we had to learn to ignore the germ-trading as we all sipped greedily from the same water jugs at the end of the fields. And we had to act promptly to provide first aid on more than one occasion when a hoe flew out of a person's hand and gashed the head of a fellow bean-walker. On more than one occasion, various wildlife, including rabbits, birds and deer would be resting in the shade of the soybean bushes and be startled by our abrupt appearance in the row of beans. Of course, they weren't the only ones startled. After the shock of the animal's quick movements and hasty retreat just mere feet from one of us, we would tease each other about having to change our underwear.

Due to the bean-walking business, my poor mother never did get to name her last baby. My youngest sister was born in July during the heart of the bean-walking season. The whole crew came up with the name for the new baby while we were out in the fields. Dad reported our decision to Mom when he went to see her in the hospital. Since he was working with us and participated in the discussion we all had, Mom never had a chance. Maybe someday she'll get a granddaughter named Ellen, a name she always liked but never got to use.

I guess I have to appreciate the work ethic instilled in all of us during those torturous hours in the fields. But every summer, I still find myself breathing a sigh of relief each time I drive by a thriving bean field full of mustard, thistles, and velvet-leaf and know that I don't have to be one of the laborers cleaning those weeds out. Heck, now all I have to labor over is being a full-time mom, a full-time wife, and working a full-time professional job. A piece of cake!

Patricia and her friends taking a break in the bean field

*Owatonna resident Patricia Kniefel was a contributing guest editorial writer for several years to the **Owatonna People's Press** newspaper.*

The Life of a Newspaper Carrier
By Patricia Kniefel

One of the less than enviable jobs assigned to me and to each of my siblings, in turn, was that of a newspaper carrier. We each spent a couple of our elementary years carrying the afternoon edition of the county paper, delivered every day but Sunday. The job was somewhat rewarding, that is, if the customers were considerate and appreciative.

On the walk home from school in Sherburn each day, I had to grab my bundle of 48 newspapers at the local drop-off site that was our one and only drugstore in town. I lugged the papers two blocks to my home, where I folded and packed them for delivery in a big, clunky, over-the-shoulder bag. The route I inherited from my older brother, who became too busy with sports, was the far southeast corner of town. I'd start out on the route around 4 p.m., and I imagine I walked a couple of miles by the time all the papers got delivered, which included a stop at several different farm homes on the outskirts of the community.

At best, that hour or so of walking the route each day was a time of fertile imaginings. Long and thoughtful contemplation of my young and naïve view of the world was not unusual. I would dream of my future, what my husband would be like, how many children I would have and what their names would be. I would dream of the anticipated excitement of going to college and living in a big city someday, working at an exciting job and meeting interesting people. At that time, my small hometown community was just a steppingstone to be tolerated until I was old enough to leave and make my place in the world.

When the weather was pleasant and the sun was shining, the job was tolerable. But Minnesota weather can be downright nasty, and winter nastiness can last for days and weeks. Many times I trudged that route in the deepening dusk of winter feeling that I was the only soul on earth. Not a car was traveling and not another person could be seen anywhere in my visible horizon. My shadow lay deep in the setting sun as winter daylight shortened and darkness crept in. My footprints were often the only ones in the deepening snow, and I made the only human sound as I trudged down the lanes to throw newspapers inside doors or mailboxes while the wind whistled piteously through the bare branches above me.

Miniature icicles would hang on my eyelashes above my scarfed face. My gloved hands and booted feet would be numb with cold as I'd gaze at the windows of homes glowing with warm, yellow light. Those moments of darkening day, and cold, solitary hours were some of the loneliest times of my young life. On many of those cheerless days, I felt small, insignificant, and unappreciated in an unforgiving wintry world. I would rush through the route as quickly as possible, pushing away those feelings and running the last few yards to my home, where I saw those same welcoming lights in the kitchen where my mom was busy preparing our evening meal. It was always a comforting sight.

In contrast to those gloomy winter days, Christmas time was gratefully different for most newspaper carriers. It was great fun to discover a small wrapped gift with my name on it in the mailbox or to be invited inside that toasty warm, glowing home for a quick hot chocolate and holiday cookies. People were kind, and I greatly appreciated their friendliness. When returning to the outside, those eerie silhouettes cast by the street lights were not quite so frightening, and the route seemed not nearly so weary and long for that lonely 10-year-old paper carrier.

I have an especially vivid memory of delivering the newspaper one winter afternoon to a very kind, elderly gentlemen who lived on one of the farthest streets on the route. He lived in a basement home and requested I bring the newspaper down to him after knocking on the door and walking down steps to his living area. He would always be sitting in his easy chair, watching the news and waiting for his paper. He would greet me with a smile and pass along a few kind words. He was one of my favorite customers.

On this one particular day, I proceeded as usual. I knocked, opened the door, and went down the steps. My gentleman customer did not hear me walk in. He had fallen asleep in his chair. The TV was still blaring and the house was toasty warm. I did not have the heart to wake him so I left the newspaper lying in his lap and tiptoed out the door.

The next day, before I headed out on my paper route, my mother asked if I had heard that my elderly customer had been found, passed away, sitting in his favorite TV chair. Even now, I can still feel the profound grief

I experienced upon hearing that news. I have no doubt that my kind and gentle customer had already been deceased when I delivered the paper to him. I never told my mother or anyone else about that incident. It was an event in my life that I felt compelled to hold on to and deal with in my own way. However, my memories of that man always remained fond and tender.

It seems to me that we have very few of those young door-to-door newspaper carriers left. Our daily newspaper is currently delivered by an adult who drives his car in the driveway and throws the paper out his window onto our sidewalk. I'm not sure that any parents this day and age would even allow their young child to walk alone for fear of abduction or wrongdoing. Times do certainly change. But what unique experiences we all have and can all jot down for future generations to smile about, laugh about and contemplate for history's sake.

*The main street of Sherburn today, population 1060. Photo courtesy of the **Martin County Star** newspaper, circulation 1214. Everybody gets the **Star!***

The Fire in Esquagamah
By Mary Murphy Ottum

It was a cold, blustery Saturday in January of 1920 up in Esquagahma near Aitkin. My mother, Hazel Crabtree Murphy, had gotten up early that morning. She fixed breakfast and we ate. She and Miss Olive Harrington, the teacher who boarded with us, had carried in snow to melt in a washtub on the heater that morning. After heating the water for washing, my mother and Miss Harrington washed the rugs and a few clothes and hung them on the line. The cold air immediately froze the rugs stiff as boards. Then Mother and Miss Harrington decided to walk to the mailbox out on Highway 35, three miles away.

My dad, Ervin Ravell Murphy, finished the outside chores, came in about 10 o'clock, and put some wood in the barrel stove. We were burning Tamarack logs that winter, which burns very hot. After Dad banked the fire in the heater, he went down to the horse barn. He was going to turn a horse loose for me to ride. It was my everyday chore to climb on her back and ride down to the swamp, chop a hole in the ice and drive the cows to water.

Our house didn't have a chimney; it had only a stovepipe. The wind, which had begun blowing hard early in the morning, was whipping the stovepipe back and forth so much it was working the pipes apart at the point where the pipes overlapped. The stove was roaring, and the hot sparks were shooting up the stovepipe to the roof as the stovepipe came apart. The sparks began falling out between the roof and the attic floor, where the pipes had separated, and that started the fire in the attic. Then the sparks caught the ceiling on fire.

I was getting ready to go out to the barn, but first I had to go upstairs for my coat. I had to climb a wooden ladder to get upstairs. When I reached the upstairs landing, sparks from the stovepipe starting falling around me. When I looked up I could see the house was on fire so I went back down the ladder without getting my coat.

I hollered to my brother, Everett, in the living room and told him to go tell Dad the house was on fire. Well, he went out and he just went, "Yoo-hoo," but he didn't tell Dad that we needed help right now. Everett went back into the house, sat on the floor and started taking his shoes and stockings off. He had been sliding down hill, and his clothes were wet.

I came down the stairs and I said, "Is Dad coming?"

He said, "He went back in the barn."

I said, "You kids get your shoes and stockings on, grab your coats and go to the horse barn." It was a good two blocks to the barn. "You stay there and tell Dad he's got to get up here and help me. The house is on fire!" They just kind of giggled at me. I said, "Well, burn up then!"

I went outside and let out a blood-curdling scream. When my dad came out of the barn, I screamed, "The house is on fire!" He said he could see the flames were going up in the sky from where he stood. Dad came to the house, and we tried to get things out, but instead of taking out the small things he grabbed the big dining room table and started to pull it out through the doorway. It lost a wheel in the crack of the floor and the table lodged there. He couldn't get it out of the way. He tried to tip it up and back, but he couldn't move it. Then he crawled over the table back into the house and took a window out. He tried to throw things out through the window. The wind was blowing so hard he couldn't do much. Neither he nor I ever thought of getting the "dresser drawer" out. That was one of those things they preached to us every time they left the house. "If the house gets on fire take that dresser drawer out and put it the outhouse," because it was quite a ways from the house. "And get the boys out." I got the boys out, but I didn't get the dresser drawer, and what money we had, burned up with the house. Dad grabbed some papers lying on top of the organ and threw them out through the window. He did save some important papers. He pushed those things out the window to me. Then he collapsed from the smoke.

I got him out, but I don't know how. It had to be the Lord helping me because he weighed at least 180 pounds. I finally got ahold of him, and I was tugging and tugging trying to pull him.

I hollered at him, "Push with your feet! Push with your feet!" I kept pulling, and I finally got him out through the window into the snow. I didn't get him too far from the house, maybe about seven or eight feet away, when the roof, instead of falling inward, split and slid outward. The roof was burning right there by his feet. I covered him with snow and tried to bring him to. I slapped him in the face with snow again and again. Finally, he got where he could breathe again.

The cellar under the house was full of food for the winter. There was also meat in several barrels just inside the back porch. There was venison and pork in the barrels. Dad had recently butchered a calf so there was also veal. What a loss! Several barrels of frozen meat–gone. We never thought of pulling the meat away from the porch. We could have easily rolled the barrels, away from the house. The roof came down over the porch trapping the barrels and Dad hollered, "Oh, God, the meat!" But by then there was nothing we could do about it.

We had nothing left. I didn't have clothes, and I didn't have a coat. The man we had been renting the house from had given me his daughter's coat. He said his girls couldn't wear it anymore. To me it was a new coat, and I was so happy to have it. But that, too, burned up in the house.

Dad said, "We can't do any more here. I don't know what we are going to do." He wanted to know if I had turned any of the cows loose. I said, "No, I didn't get out there." He went out to check the cows in the barn. He came back after he had given them hay. We didn't get any water to them that day.

Then he went back to the barn, hitched up the horses and put us on the sled, covered us with hay and said, "I'm going to have to take you down to your grandfather's." My grandfather was C.W. Crabtree.

I said, "Dad, why can't we take those rugs off of the line? They're frozen, but if you put them on top of the hay, wouldn't that help keep the wind from going through the hay and keep us a little warmer?"

Well, he didn't know if it would do any good, but he said, "We'll take them off of the line." And he took the rugs and the clothes that were on the line and threw that on the top of the hay to keep the wind off.

We started down one of the logging roads along Esquagamah Lake to Grandpa's house. As we were going down the road, we saw tracks that crossed the road where our teacher, Olive Harrington, and my mother had walked on a cow trail back toward the house. Dad ran along the trail after them yelling and hollering. He finally headed them off, and they came back and rode to Grandpa Crabtree's house with us.

Dad told them, "The house is gone, no use trying to go there. Got to get these kids to their grandparents and get them something to wear; they ain't got any fit clothes on." I didn't have a thing because my clothes were burned so badly to my body. He had got us in the sled and got us covered with hay and the wet rugs. That's the way we went for two miles down the tote road to my grandfather's house. We saved only what was on the clothesline.

That night and for many nights after, I slept on a pallet on the floor next to my grandmother's bed. She slept with her hand on me, and I guess I was shivering. Every little while she'd shake me, "Come on, Mary, you're all right. You're with your grandma."

We moved to Swatara that year and back to Esquagamah in 1927. I didn't get over the fire experience for a long, long time. I could tell when there was a fire nearby. I didn't know where, but I knew there was a fire. When we'd go into town I'd tell them, "There's a fire and the whistle is going to be a blowing!"

"You don't know what you are talking about; get busy with your work," they'd tell me. Then the fire whistle would start to blow.

Mary Murphy Ottum died in Aitkin in 2005 at age 93. Swatara native Stacy Vellas, a regular **Minnesota Memories** *contributor, interviewed and transcribed her stories in 1996 and submitted them for this volume. Stacy's mother was Olive Harrington, Mary's beloved teacher.*

Esquagamah Country Teachers
By Mary Murphy Ottum

My first teacher was Miss Olive Harrington, and I remember her so well. I was only 8 when she came to board at our house in the fall of 1920. The schoolhouse was near Esquagamah Lake, about a mile from our house.

Miss Harrington was a good teacher and a very nice person. We didn't have a school when I was small so I never did get the first two grades and the phonics that you usually get. I missed kindergarten completely. Although I was 8, she started me out in first grade. She taught me reading, writing and arithmetic. She had a lot of patience. If I didn't get it right, we tried it until I did get it.

She taught me how to pronounce words and I had poems to learn. She was the one who taught me how to introduce people. One time my aunt came to the house to visit. A gentleman who was hunting in the area walked through our yard. He was cold so he stopped at our house to get warm. Miss Harrington had told me how to introduce people. I was to introduce him to my aunt and explain to her what relation Mr. Smith was to me. He was my great uncle.

My mother had had a miscarriage. She was in bed when the neighbors came to visit. When they came in, I said, "Mr. and Mrs. Nosmoke, they are friends of ours, please meet my great uncle and aunt, Mr. Kilpatrick and Mrs. Kilpatrick." They said they never heard a child my age who could introduce people so nicely. It was because Miss Harrington taught me.

We said the Pledge of Allegiance every morning. Then we had a little club, and we learned how to make motions like you do in parliamentary procedure. There were only the two of us. Isn't that funny? Miss Harrington spent a lot of time with us teaching us different things.

Miss Harrington walked down to the school in the early morning. She would start the fire and get the school warmed up before we got there. In the evening sometimes we walked home together. Sometimes she sent us on ahead and she came a little later.

One day when I walked to school just before Christmas I had to stop to make arrangements for the teacher to be paid. First I took an order from the teacher to the clerk. The next morning I had to pick up the check and take it to the teacher. We were told to walk two or three children together and never leave anyone to walk alone in the wilderness because there were wild animals in those early days. We didn't have to worry about bears because bears hibernated during the winter but wolves, foxes and lynx roamed the forest looking for food.

That day they went on and left me. As I walked home I could feel something following me. As I came to the cedar swamp near home I could feel two spots just burning into my back. I didn't know what was following me. I stopped and stood still. I couldn't move. I tried to turn and look back, but I could only turn my head so far, and then I had to turn and look ahead.

As I passed our neighbor's house, the man living there came out his door. He turned quickly and rushed back in the house. He came out with a gun and pointed it at me and shot. I thought he was going to shoot me. It was then I turned around and saw the lynx behind me darting off through the woods. I was shivering so hard he brought me into the house. His wife gave me some cocoa, and they told me I was all right. He said that when he came out he saw the lynx behind me. It was crouched and ready to pounce.

After our house burned, we moved to Swatara, and we rode the bus to school. We all came down with chicken pox. I was the last of our family to catch chicken pox. The rest of the kids missed school because they were sick before Christmas. I didn't miss any school because I had chicken pox during vacation.

In 1927, we returned to Esquagamah. We had a teacher named Miss Lamb from St. Cloud, and she lived with us too. She liked to listen to a bachelor singing on the telephone at night. Everybody else went to bed. She stayed up and listened to him sing away into the night. The next morning we had to call her and call her to wake up and get out of bed. When we all got to school, the teacher would put her head down on the desk and go to sleep.

One morning she rang the bell for us to take our seats. We opened our books to study, and she put her head down on her desk. After a while when we needed help with our school work, we called her but she wouldn't wake up. We thought that was funny. She didn't wake up, and she didn't wake up. I went to her desk and listened once. Did she die? I listened and I heard her breathing. She was snoring. I went back to my seat.

After a while we got hungry. It was noon, and she was still asleep. We ate our lunch. Then we tried to wake her. We couldn't wake her. Finally, it was starting to get dark so we went home. She had slept all day. She finally woke up and came home after dark.

After supper Miss Lamb would pick up the phone and listen to the bachelor sing opera songs. The telephone would be tied up for hours. One night my dad said he wanted to call my uncle about business. Miss Lamb was on the phone. He told her she had to get off the phone and that she had been on it long enough. She said, "Oh, he's singing so beautifully!" I can still see her face when she was telling Dad that.

Dad went outdoors, and pretty soon she was standing there when the phone went dead and there was no singing. Dad had gone outside and disconnected the wire. After a while she went to bed. Then Dad reconnected the wire and called my uncle.

Young Olive Harrington

In the 1980s I found the address and phone number of Olive Harrington, my first teacher. I called her in California and we talked. She remembered me, and wanted to know if I had gone through high school. I had to tell her, "No, I didn't. I didn't even get through the seventh grade." She said it was too bad I couldn't finish because I was very capable as a child. We corresponded for a while until she couldn't write anymore.

Gear Head
By Don Matejcek

In the Owatonna High School Class of 1961, I was one of the gear heads–you know, the guy who is always fiddling with cars and trucks. What the heck, I'd still be considered a gear head because I've made a living working on cars and trucks. Other than three years I spent fixing helicopters for Uncle Sam, that is how I've spent my adult life.

In the summer of 1955, I bought a flat head V-8 engine just so I could take it apart and see how it worked. In the summer of 1956, I bought a Model-A Ford pickup with big ideas of making it into a hot rod. I bought an Oldsmobile V-8 engine and put it into the pickup, but when school started I had to sell all that stuff so I could quit my odd jobs and go out for wrestling in 1956.

In the fall of 1960 I bought a 1946 Plymouth with a flat head 6-cylinder engine, and thinking about that car brings up memories of the drag strips in Minnesota. We were always going out into the country on blacktop roads to drag, but then we heard about the first drag strip up in New Brighton. I started going up there in 1956. We saw the start of the muscle car era, and we'd watch the manufacturers battle it out.

I have many drag strip stories. A fellow who worked at the Owatonna Ford dealership had a 1957 Mercury with a super charger. The charger was belt driven. One time he wound that engine up so tight that right in front of the grandstand, the belt came off. It ate a hole in the hood and shot out like a missile. The original New Brighton strip ran from west to east. When Interstate 35 was put in, they tried to make sure a car could stop before it got to the freeway by putting a dirt mound on the east end. That didn't work so they had to turn the strip around.

One guy from the Cities found out that the dirt mound didn't work when he lost his brakes and ran into the dirt pile. They pulled his car back to the parking lot and he went home to get his daddy's 1957 supercharged Thunderbird. The first car he came up against was a 1957 Chevy, driven by a big guy who didn't like to lose. If he was in danger of getting beat, he would start bouncing back and forth on the steering wheel. It looked like he was trying to help push the car down the track with his weight.

We still had flagmen at that time. When the flagman dropped the green flag, I thought the big fellow was going to break off the steering wheel as he watched the T-bird pull away from him. After that run, the guy in the Chevy wouldn't let the T-bird go back to the parking lot until they ran again. It was bye-bye T-bird again.

I believe it was the summer of 1958 when Minnesota Dragways opened in Coon Rapids. At first it had flagmen, but then it became more modern and got lights for starting. One of my favorite stories about that strip involved a guy from Owatonna with his 1957 Merc. He took that engine out and put it into a 1940 Ford coupe that sounded pretty mean with its supercharger whining. In his class there was a little Willys named Ramona the Rainmaker. It had a Chevy V-8 engine. They were always pretty close until one Sunday Ramona started winning every time. The guy with the '40 Ford didn't show up for a couple of weeks. When he did and they backed it off the trailer, it sounded like the world's largest vacuum cleaner. He had stuck another 4-barrel carb and supercharger onto this Merc engine. He didn't have any problems with Ramona until they modified something on Ramona and the battle was back on.

This brings me back to the 1946 Plymouth that reminded me of drag strips. I dragged it with the flat head 6-cylindar engine and won a couple of trophies. Then I got to thinking, if a 6-cylinder would do this well, an 8-cylinder would be better. WRONG. A friend and I stuffed a hemi under the hood. I shouldn't say under the hood, as it took us about three months to figure out how to modify the hood to even bolt it back on. I was so broke that when the battery went bad, my friend had to stop by every morning and give me a push to get started. At school I'd park on a hill so I could roll it down the hill to get started. Every time I took it to the drag strip, I'd break down and have to get pulled home. After that I bought a customized 1956 Chevy. Here I was, a Ford man with Ford almost tattooed on my chest, driving a Chevy. Dragging with that was just that, a drag. Every time I'd drag, I'd break down.

In the fall of 1961, I took up SCUBA diving. This took a lot of my spare time, and didn't cost nearly as much as dragging. Then Uncle Sam came looking for me so I just drove beaters waiting for my call up.

Owatonna resident Don Matejcek has been a contributor since 2002.

Victory Can Be Painful
By Robert D. "Cobb" Knutson

The Albert Lea Parks and Recreation Department provided a popular variety of activities and competitions for kids during the summers when I was growing up, and every week they had some kind of contest. Whether your game was softball, box hockey, badminton or checkers, there were local playground playoffs followed by city-wide tournaments, often with ribbons or prizes for the champions.

In June of 1955, they held an ice cream eating contest to help celebrate Freeborn County Dairy Days. We didn't really have a park on the east side of town, but we read about the contest in the paper and thought it would be fun to compete. We rode our bikes to North Side Park to see if we could participate, and we were happy when we found out that it would be okay.

The playground supervisor told us the rules, and at first it sounded like a dream come true for a kid on a hot summer day. All we had to do was eat two pints of ice cream as fast as possible. The ice cream came in a brick, and we were supposed to just pick it up with our hands and dive into it. The winner would be the one who finished first.

Well, it must have been my lucky day because I won. My prize was the chance to travel about a mile to Morin Park on the west side of town to compete with the winners from other parks for the all-city ice cream eating championship.

After a very short period of recuperation, I hopped back on my bike and arrived at Morin Park an hour later, and I learned that the rules for this final round of the contest were the same. The first person to finish two pint-sized bricks of solid, hard, strawberry ice cream would be named city champion.

The first pint went fast, but by the time I started on the second one, it was torture. My lips, hands, tongue, throat and teeth were frozen for the second time that day. I was sticky all over and stuffed to the gills because by this time I had consumed four pint-sized bricks of strawberry ice cream in one afternoon.

But despite the pain, I persevered. I didn't win first place, but I did come in second. Richard Ponto, age 14, was crowned Albert Lea's 1955 ice cream eating champ by finishing his two pints in 2 minutes and 17 seconds. I was right behind him though.

We each won something, but I can't remember what it was. The next day, our picture appeared in the paper, and though we were victorious, we all looked a little sick. I don't think I had any cravings for ice cream for a long time after that day.

Front Row, Bob Olson, Cobb Knutson, Bill Myers
All winners–all a little sick

Cobb Knutson is a retired state trooper who worked for more than thirty years in Minnesota law enforcement. He enjoys fishing, old cars, history and travel. He has four daughters and seven grandchildren. This story first appeared in the book ***Albert Lea Remembers,*** *published by the Friends of the Albert Lea Library in 2004.*

About Minnesota Memories 7

I have always considered myself a Minnesotan. While living in other states, I enjoyed getting together with fellow Minnesotans to share stories about life in the North Star State. These stories not only entertained, but they refreshed and restored whatever it was about my mind and soul that needed refreshment and restoration.

In 2000, I was teaching in Maryland, and across the hall was another native Minnesotan, Kathy Megyeri. One day, after Kathy sold a story to the *Chicken Soup* publishers, I said, "Somebody should compile a book of stories about life in Minnesota. Every Minnesotan has at least one good, true story or recollection, and a compilation of all those stories would make a terrific book." We pitched that idea to a few publishers of regional books, and they pitched it right back.

After recovering from this rejection, we decided that we would take it upon ourselves to compile and publish a book of extraordinary stories by ordinary Minnesota folks. When we contacted old friends, only a few responded and sent stories because many doubted that we would actually publish a book. Undaunted, we confounded those skeptics, wrote some of our own stories, combined them with a few we received from other people, and published *Minnesota Memories* in 2001.

I traveled more than 10,000 miles that first summer, from Grand Marais to Austin and from Adrian to Winona, talking to newspaper reporters and radio interviewers about my *Minnesota Memories* mission. I spoke at county fairs, schools, class reunions, book stores, trade shows, service clubs, church groups and historical societies, inviting ordinary people to send their extraordinary stories for *Minnesota Memories 2*.

The response was terrific. Since then, I have traveled thousands of additional miles meeting people all over Minnesota, collecting and publishing hundreds of their true stories in seven volumes. My youngest contributor was 9 years old, and my oldest was nearly 100.

Thank you for supporting this project by purchasing or reading this book. I hope you had fun and that these stories triggered some of your own Minnesota Memories. Every Minnesotan or former Minnesotan with a true story to tell is welcome to submit it for the next volume. Everybody loves a good story, and stories love to be shared.

Joan Claire Graham, Purveyor of Memories

Writers from these towns submitted stories for *Minnesota Memories 7*.
Is there a story from your town?

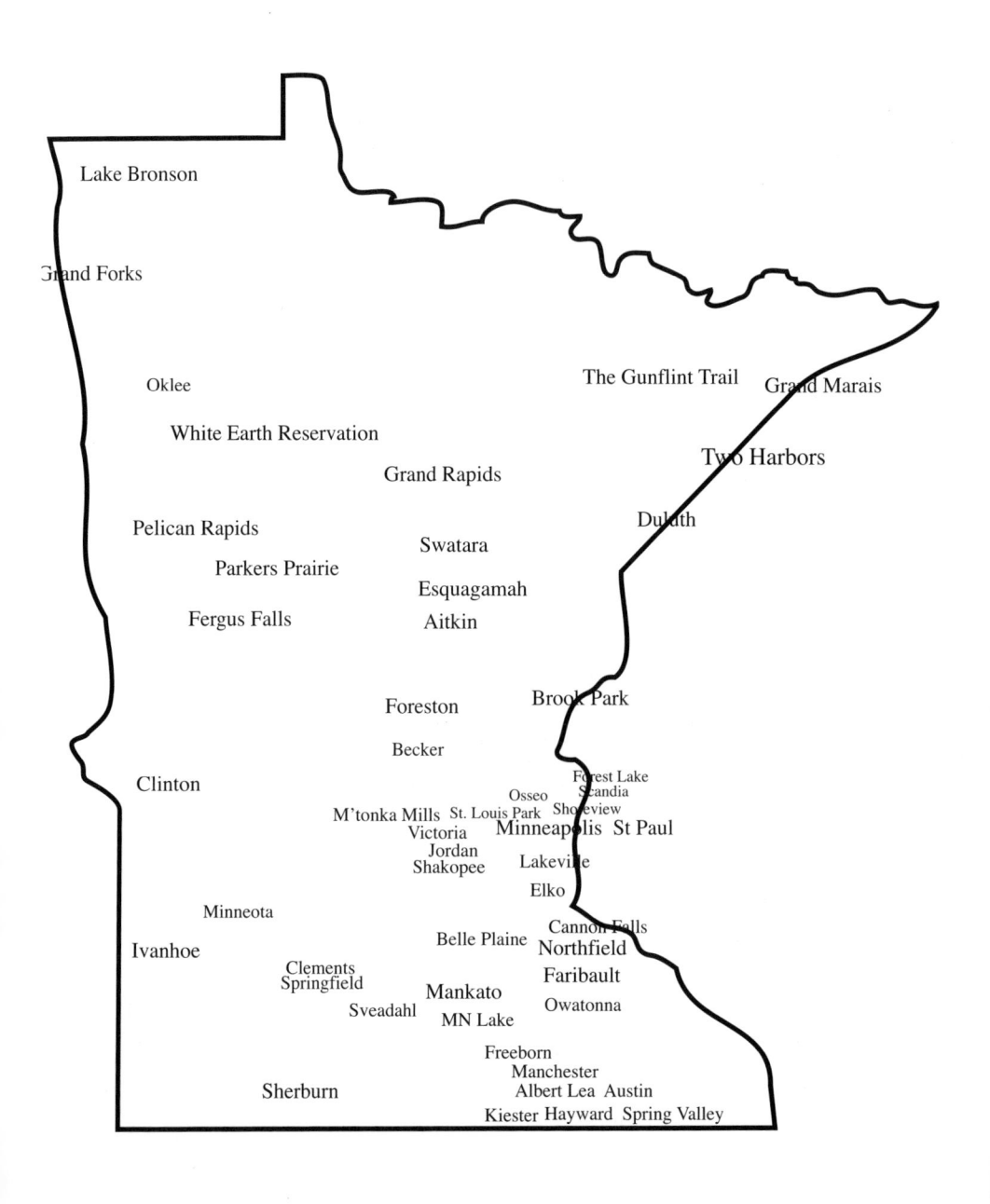

Lake Bronson
Grand Forks
Oklee
White Earth Reservation
The Gunflint Trail
Grand Marais
Grand Rapids
Two Harbors
Pelican Rapids
Swatara
Duluth
Parkers Prairie
Esquagamah
Fergus Falls
Aitkin
Foreston
Brook Park
Becker
Forest Lake
Osseo
Scandia
Clinton
M'tonka Mills St. Louis Park Shoreview
Victoria Minneapolis St Paul
Jordan
Shakopee Lakeville
Elko
Minneota
Cannon Falls
Belle Plaine Northfield
Ivanhoe
Clements
Faribault
Springfield
Mankato Owatonna
Sveadahl MN Lake
Freeborn
Manchester
Sherburn Albert Lea Austin
Kiester Hayward Spring Valley